THE MATHESON TRUST

The principal objective of The Matheson Trust is to promote the study of comparative religion from the point of view of the underlying harmony of the great religious and philosophical traditions of the world. This objective is being pursued through such means as audio-visual media, the support and sponsorship of lecture series and conferences, the creation of a website, collaboration with film production companies and publishing companies as well as the Trust's own series of publications.

THE GREAT WAR OF THE DARK AGE

धर्मे चार्थे च कामे च मोक्षे च भरतर्षभ ।
यदिहास्ति तदन्यत्र यन्नेहास्ति न तत्क्वचित् ॥

O Bull of the Bhārata, regarding the goals of man

—conformity to order, material wealth, love and deliverance—

everything which is in this text can also be found elsewhere.

What is not here cannot be found anywhere else.

The Great War of the Dark Age

Keys to the *Mahābhārata*

Dominique Wohlschlag

translated from the French by
Deborah Bell

THE MATHESON TRUST
For the Study of Comparative Religion

Originally published as
Clés pour le Mahābhārata,
by Infolio Éditions, Gollion, Switzerland, 2013.

This first English edition published by

The Matheson Trust
PO Box 336
56 Gloucester Road
London SW7 4UB, UK

www.themathesontrust.org

ISBN: 978 1 908092 17 5

British Library Cataloguing-in-Publication Data.
A catalogue record for this book is
available from the British Library.

Typeset by the publishers in Baskerville 10 Pro.

Cover: detail from the *Razmnāmah* or 'Persian Mahābhārata'
© The British Library Board, Or. 12076, f. 76r.
Cover design by Susana Marín.

Contents

Preface

The *Mahābhārata*, India's great epic, is a monumental literary work which is, to say the least, overwhelming: first of all because of its sheer size comprising nearly ten thousand pages of daunting and strictly rhythmic verse; then the endless number of gods and heroes it portrays; the abundance of myths taken from ancient sources which it then develops, alters and reshuffles; its long didactic digressions and the considerable influence it has had on the arts; and above all the religious and spiritual role it has played for more than two millennia, and indeed which it continues to play, within the framework of that still miraculously living and multifaceted tradition which is Hinduism. Yet these exceptional and formidable qualities do it rather a disservice. For few present day Western readers, whether fond of classical literature, curious to discover the world's literary masterpieces or avid for oriental wisdom though they may be, have ever read more than brief summaries of it. At the most, lovers of oriental 'flavours' (*rasa*) will have so far been content with tasting here and there a few morsels, admiring its iconography, going to a few Indian plays or seeing one or two Western or oriental films on the subject.

Certainly, after their first halting steps, some excellent Indologists, above all since the second half of the 20th century, have contributed significantly to making inroads into this vast subject and shedding new light on it. Thus there is a gradual tendency in academic circles to do the epic greater justice and finally give it its rightful place in the artistic, intellectual and spiritual heritage of mankind. Unfortunately the works of scholars who apply themselves to this task are often not much less dense than their subject, riddled as they are with scholarly references and sophisticated hypotheses, and they are hardly ever read except by the specialists they are addressed to. That is why we have risen to the challenge of attempting to offer to the wider public a sort of introduction to the *Mahābhārata* while making as few demands on the reader as possible.

The present work takes up a certain number of themes that we had already begun exploring in a loose fashion in *The Queen and the Avatar* (2017). It inevitably contains a number of repetitions which we believe nonetheless to be limited to the essential. However, here we have followed a more systematic method which makes use of modern critical Orientalism whenever we have judged it necessary. While the traditional Hindu approach is certainly sufficient in itself, we believe that the epic has definitely nothing to lose by being scrutinised by outsiders. As long as the authors who approach this work respect its real genius, it can only gain in universal recognition. It is nevertheless to the *sanātana-dharma*, to the perennial tradition of India, that we must leave the last word.

A note on the transcription of Sanskrit terms

Sanskrit vowels are pronounced very much like Italian vowels, with the exception of the short *a*, which is pronounced like the *u* in the English word 'but'; the long *ā* is pronounced like the *a* in 'father'.

As for the consonants, a reasonable approximation will be obtained by pronouncing *c* as in 'church', *j* as in 'jungle', *ṣ* as in 'shun', *s* as in 'sun', *ś* as something halfway between the other two s's.

The aspirated consonants should be pronounced distinctly; *bh* as in 'cab-horse', *dh* as in 'mad-house', *gh* as in 'dog-house', *ph* as in 'top-hat', and *th* as in 'goat-herd'.

ṛ is a vowel, pronounced midway between *ri* as in 'rivet' and *er* as in 'father'.

[From: Wendy Doniger O'Flaherty, *Hindu Myths*, Penguin Books, 1975.]

NB: the proper names of places and personalities of modern India are given in their usual form without diacritical marks.

1

What is the *Mahābhārata*?

APART FROM THE *Bhagavad-gītā*, which is often published separately as a short extract from it, the *Mahābhārata* in its entirety, literally the *Great (War) of the Bhārata*, is perhaps the most famous text of Indian literature. The Bhārata are the descendants of Bharata (as indicated by the lengthening of the first ā), an eminent member of the 'lunar' dynasty who once reigned in the north of India and whose origins can be traced back to Candra, the moon.[1] Indians to this day call their country Bhārata, or Bhārata-varṣa, the kingdom of Bhārata, in Sanskrit, as well as in all their vernacular languages. The word 'India' is nothing but a foreign name given by Westerners who, from the time of Alexander the Great onwards, described in this way the area which for them was beyond the river Indus. In essence, the *Mahābhārata* retells the story of an important dynastic conflict which took place in a mythical time in the history of the family

---

[1] All the planets in the etymological meaning of wandering stars, therefore including the sun and the moon, are in Indian mythology masculine deities. The name *Candra*, The Silver One, is close, via the Indo-European, to the English cinders.

of Bharata. It is an immense epic recital full of twists and turns, which is replete with narrative and didactic asides, and teeming with an incredible number of people of all walks of life variously woven into the general dramatic framework.

Here, to start with, is a short summary:[2]

ॐ

Śāntanu, the king of the lunar Bhārata dynasty, reigns over a large territory situated in the north of India. His capital is Hāstinapura, the Town of the Elephant, on the banks of the Ganges. Desirous of obtaining an heir, he first of all has an affair with the goddess Gaṅgā, who gives him a strong and virtuous son called Bhīṣma. But the goddess leaves him and he falls madly in love with Satyavatī, the daughter of the King of the Fish, who agrees to give her to Śāntanu on the express condition that it will be one of her sons, in other words a son of his own line, who will inherit the kingdom. Out of reverence for his father, the magnanimous Bhīṣma, legitimate heir to the throne, renounces power and even marriage in order to avoid any conflict which could be caused by the birth of direct offspring from the older line of the dynasty he represents.

Satyavatī thus marries Śāntanu and gives him two sons who die before coming to the throne, and what is more, before they can even beget descendants. In despair at this, she confesses that she has already had,

2 The reader keen to better acquaint himself with the details of the story is invited to look at the works cited under *Mahābhārata* in the bibliography.

thanks to a clandestine affair with a Brahmin, a son called Kṛṣṇa Dvaipāyana. This dirty and unkempt hermit will, under the name of Vyāsa, become the author of the *Mahābhārata*. She gets her husband to agree that Vyāsa sleep with the two sisters who had been married to her younger son, now deceased, in an attempt to save the line of the King of the Fish.

With the first of the wives of his half-brother, Vyāsa begets Dhṛtarāṣṭra, who is unfortunately born blind, because his mother, Ambikā, disgusted by the repulsive looks of the hermit, had shut her eyes during intercourse. With the second wife, Ambālikā, he engenders Pāṇḍu, who is as pale as death for, alerted to the mishap of her sister, the young woman had kept her eyes open at the fateful moment, but could not prevent herself turning white with fear. Vyāsa did not stop there, but engendered with a serving woman a third child, who became the wise Vidura.

On the death of Śāntanu, the kingdom is initially bequeathed to Pāṇḍu, the second son, because it is considered a bad omen for the kingdom to be ruled by a blind king. A short time after his coronation, Pāṇḍu marries Kuntī, the future aunt of Kṛṣṇa, who belongs to a distant branch of the family, and the beautiful Mādrī, the daughter of the king of Madra. Unfortunately, he becomes the victim of a curse which condemns him to die the moment he has sexual relations with a woman. So Kuntī reveals a secret to him: she has a *mantra*, a sacred formula, which permits her to have children with any god that she invokes. Pāṇḍu agrees to this compromise on condition that it is he who will choose the gods who beget his descendants himself. Thanks to these supernatural means, and under the orders of her husband, Kuntī first of all gives birth to Yudhiṣṭhira, born of the god Dharma (the Law), then to Bhīma, born of the god Vāyu (the Wind), and finally to Arjuna, born of the god Indra (the Rain, Thunder, and King of the gods). Then she transmits the *mantra* to her co-wife, who becomes in her turn the mother of Nakula and Sahadeva, the twin boys of the Aśvin gods (the Horsemen, twin gods who are divine keepers of the wealth of the gods and their physicians). These five brothers make up the Pāṇḍava clan who will stay united to the end, but what no one knows apart from Kuntī, is that she has already had, before her marriage, a son with the god Sūrya (the Sun). However, she abandoned him, and he was adopted by a married couple of the charioteer caste who named him Karṇa.

For his part, the blind Dhṛtarāṣṭra marries Gāndhārī, who takes a vow to live her entire life with a blindfold round her eyes in order to be equal to her husband. A little later on, Gāndhārī gives birth, very painfully, to a hundred sons who are born in one go from a ball of iron which she carried for two years in her womb. The eldest is Duryodhana, who at the head of his ninety-nine brothers becomes the leader of the Kaurava clan who are opposed to the Pāṇḍava.

In spite of the curse he lives under, Pāṇḍu ends in succumbing to the charms of Mādrī and dies making love to her. Weeping uncontrollably, the young woman throws herself on the king's funeral pyre, and Kuntī adopts her two children. The kingdom is conferred on Dhṛtarāṣṭra, in spite of his handicap. During his regency, the one hundred and five cousins of the two branches of the family are brought up together at the court under the direction of a master of arms, the Brahmin Droṇa.

Once the young men become adults, Dhṛtarāṣṭra is consulted to find out who will inherit the throne. The blind old man, against all expectations, chooses as crown prince not his eldest son, Duryodhana, but his nephew, Yudhiṣṭhira, who has a reputation for being a very righteous man. From then on, the ambitious Duryodhana will not cease until he has snatched away the throne that he believes to have been unjustly given to his cousin. In order to avoid an imminent conflict, it is provisionally decided to divide the kingdom in two. The town of Hāstinapura, on the Ganges, remains the capital of Dhṛtarāṣṭra and his sons, while Yudhiṣṭhira and his brothers are installed at Indraprastha, on the Yamunā.

Meanwhile, Drupada, the king of Kāśi (Bénarès), organises a tournament whose prize will be his daughter, Draupadī. All the princes attend, and it is Arjuna who wins. On returning home he calls out to his mother that he has won a contest. But Kuntī, who does not know what he has won, immediately tells him, 'share the prize with your brothers.' As she cannot go back on her words, Draupadī becomes, thanks to the strength of this oracle, the common wife of the Pāṇḍava. This polyandrous marriage is a happy one, even when later Bhīma and Arjuna have other wives.

After several unsuccessful attempts to eliminate his cousins, Duryodhana invites Yudhiṣṭhira, whose weak spot he knows full well, to a dice game in the course of which he gets his uncle, Śakuni, a notorious cheat, to play in his place. Driven on by his passion for dice, the unfortunate Yudhiṣṭhira begins by losing all his wealth, then his army and his kingdom. He then bets and loses successively his four brothers, himself, and then their common wife, Draupadī. Eager to revel in his total victory, Duryodhana asks his brother Duḥśāsana to go and fetch the young woman and strip her in front of everyone in order to humiliate his cousins. But the wretched young woman, pulled by the hair into the middle of the shocked assembly, has the presence of mind to invoke the name of Kṛṣṇa, a distant cousin of the family who reigns in a neighbouring kingdom. This cousin who is physically absent from these events is said to be an avatar—an earthly incarnation of Viṣṇu, the Supreme divinity. This identity is only sensed by some people and remains unknown to others. By means of his *māyā*, his power of illusion, Kṛṣṇa produces a miracle. He makes Draupadī's saree become endless in length as Duḥśāsana tries to pull it off, thus ridiculing her tormentors. The wife of the Pāṇḍava then points out that the game of dice was actually technically flawed: Yudhiṣṭhira had bet her when he had already lost himself! He therefore had no right to dispose of her. She thus gains from Dhṛtarāṣṭra, by way of compensation, the release of her five husbands. But they must go into exile for twelve years and stay incognito during the thirteenth before they are allowed to return.

After this long period of waiting, and in spite of all Duryodhana's attempts to flush out his cousins in order to destroy them, the Pāṇḍava are able to return to Indraprastha. But this situation cannot satisfy the insatiable Duryodhana. War threatens, in spite of Kṛṣṇa's attempts at reconciliation, when the two clans bring him in to arbitrate between them. Finally the avatar offers the two opponents a choice: either one of them can have his personal help, though without him joining in fight, and the other one will then have his army but without him. The decision falls to Arjuna, who opts for the first choice, and Kṛṣṇa's army is sent over to Duryodhana, who is overjoyed with the deal.

The war is now inevitable and lasts for eighteen days. In the midst of the intense fighting Kṛṣṇa exhorts and advises the Pāṇḍava, not without using some ruses and tricks which any soldier would find morally troubling. But these transgressions are perpetrated only because of the deceit of their enemies, especially Duryodhana's. Thus fall one after another the generals and chiefs of the Kaurava army, that is, Bhīṣma, Droṇa, Karṇa, and then Śalya. Finally Duryodhana succumbs in single combat against Bhīma, and the Pāṇḍava win, but at a terrible price. What is worse is that Droṇa's son, Aśvatthāman, one of the three remaining survivors of the Kaurava, manages to find a way to massacre the survivors of the Pāṇḍava army in their sleep, including the five sons of Draupadī. The only ones to escape his vengeance are the five brothers and two other soldiers. Aśvatthāman, wishing to complete his work of destruction, targets Arjuna's unborn grandchild, Parikṣit, the last hope of the dynasty, who is still in the womb of his mother Uttarā. But Kṛṣṇa succeeds in stopping him before returning home to Dvārakā. Yudhiṣṭhira can now reign unchallenged over the kingdom of Bhārata. Thirty-six years later, having now grown old, he leaves the throne to Parikṣit, Arjuna's grandchild, and retires to the Himalaya with his wife and four brothers who all die on the way. Eventually, after a final trial during which he refuses to give up the dog who accompanies him, and who is none other, in this modest guise, than a manifestation of his father Dharma—which at first he does not actually realise—he ascends to the heaven of Indra in his body. It is there that he finds his family, in an infernal region from where they are destined to be purified of their last sins before their glorious assumption. Parikṣit now reigns unchallenged over the kingdom of Bhārata, and is reputed to be the mythical ancestor of all present day Indians.

*

So in its form the *Mahābhārata* is what is known as an epic. It belongs to a literary genre that in India is called *itihāsa*, which means literally 'he spoke thus,' an expression that corresponds roughly to our 'once upon a time.' This word appears for the first time in one of the first *Upaniṣad*,[3] the *Chāndogyopaniṣad* (7, 1, 2), in connection with the word *purāṇa* (ancient). The *itihāsa-purāṇa*, the ancient story, is cited in fifth place after the first four *Veda* as a source of knowledge. As a result, the *Mahābhārata*, later identified with this particular *itihāsa*, is considered a fifth *Veda*, a title which shows how important this text is to the Indian consciousness.[4] This passage of the *Chāndogyopaniṣad* proves that there existed in India, before

[3] The *Upaniṣad* are relatively short texts (with the exception of two of them, of about a hundred pages each). They belong to Vedic literature, to which they bring a philosophical and metaphysical vision.

[4] The same honour has been given to the *Nāṭya-śāstra*, a very early work dedicated to the theatre, which has played an important role throughout the history of Indian concepts of art.

the appearance of an epic properly speaking, a corpus of legends which were probably recited during ceremonies that accompanied certain Vedic rites. In addition, playing on the etymology of the root *BHṚ*, meaning to carry, the *Mahābhārata* (1, 1, 208–9) declares itself to be weightier than the *Veda*: 'Once the divine seers foregathered, and on one side they hung the four *Vedas*, and on the other scale they hung *The Bhārata*; and both in size and in weight it was the heavier. Therefore, because of its size and its weight, it is called *The Mahābhārata*.'[5]

We have spoken with regard to the *itihāsa* of a literary genre, since this generic name can be extended to the *Purāṇa* [6] and even other writings such as the literature of the fables. But only one work of this immense corpus can be really compared to the *Mahābhārata*, and that is the *Rāmāyaṇa*, or *The Deeds of Rāma*, an epic hardly less famous than the *Mahābhārata* in India, though it is more widespread throughout the region of South-East Asia. Now, these two texts relate above all to the Hindu religious sect called Vaisnavism, since their principal heroes, namely Kṛṣṇa and Rāma, are two *avatāra* or 'descents' of the god Viṣṇu on earth. In the mythological chronology of the ten major avatars of Viṣṇu, which became fixed later on, Rāma's story is presented as

---

5 Cited by Danielle Feller (2004: 13) in the English translation of Van Buitenen.

6 The *Purāṇa* properly so called make up of a huge corpus of texts of a mythological character, but all are written after the *Mahābhārata*. There are eighteen major and eighteen minor works. They are for the most part very long, and feed the imagination of numerous Hindu sects, whether Vaisnavite, Śaivite or Śaktic.

belonging to a more ancient age than Kṛṣṇa's.[7] But this does not necessarily mean that the *Rāmāyaṇa* was written before the *Mahābhārata*. It could very well have come afterwards, in the sense that it is an elaboration of an episode found in the deeds of the Bhārata where the whole story of Rāma is briefly told, and its style, which is much more refined, gives credence to this interpretation. The *Rāmāyaṇa* seems to be, in effect, a more successful, homogeneous, work on the strictly literary plane, and because of this it is often not considered an *itihāsa*, or epic properly speaking, but rather an eminent and even primordial example of what is called *kāvya*, the poetry of classical Sanskrit. This view is also supported by the relative shortness of the *Rāmāyaṇa*, which is less weighed down by the digressions, slow pace and repetitions of its 'rival'. But if these 'defects' in the recitation of the deeds of the Pāṇḍava can tire and discourage the reader, they also contribute, from another point of view, to its richness and incomparable power to fascinate.

The *Mahābhārata* was composed in Sanskrit, which obliges us to say a few words on this subject. The ancient Vedic texts, which were composed over a very long period,[8] are written in an idiom which, for want of a

---

7 The list of the ten major avatars of Viṣṇu comprises several variants, and even extends to twenty-two in the *Bhāgavata-purāṇa*, one of the most important texts of the *Purāṇa*. But Rāma always precedes Kṛṣṇa.

8 The earliest compilation of Vedic hymns, the *Ṛg-veda*, attributed to a number of *ṛṣi* (literally seers), a certain number of whom were women—twenty-seven, according to tradition—, goes back, on the authority of the Indian scholars, to 4000 BC or earlier. The most ferocious of the Orientalists bring this date

specific term, is called Vedic. This language belongs to the Indo–European group and is even the most archaic form of it we know.[9] In the fourth century BC a philologist of genius named Pāṇini, probably from Lahore in present day Pakistan, wrote a famous grammar containing four thousand rules which are still learnt by heart to this day by some Brahmins concerned with maintaining the oral tradition. The language described by him on the basis of what Vedic was like in his time became from then on known as Sanskrit, *saṃskṛta*, that is to say, completed, perfect. In codifying this idiom, Pāṇini gave it its final stability. It has thus become, as a result, almost impossible to date the texts that came after this codification by purely philological criteria. This is a unique case in the history of philology, even with regard to a language reserved for religious, philosophical, scientific or literary purposes free from erosion by the vernacular. In comparison to the Vedic language, Sanskrit represents, notably in its verbal aspects, a simplification which is not devoid of artificiality. Knowing that the *Mahābhārata* was written in Sanskrit[10] implies therefore, on the

---

forward to 1200 BC, but in reality it is probably somewhere between the two dates. Coomaraswamy speaks of '1500 BC or earlier' (1979: 140). What is sure, in any case, is that the *Veda* were not written in a day and that the corpus must have been composed over several centuries.

[9] It is a sister language to Latin, Greek, Germanic idioms, Slav, Iranian, etc., rather than their common source as is sometimes said. Let us recall here that, contrary to what has so often been abusively maintained, the term 'Indo-European' refers to a linguistic order of reality (hence a cultural one) and not an ethnic one.

[10] One speaks sometimes of epic Sanskrit to characterise certain

one hand, that it was composed after the time of Pāṇini,[11] and, on the other hand, that its distribution very rapidly became pan-Indian, reflecting the Brahmanic presence which covered the entire subcontinent. Its style, stripped of the obscurities of the Vedic hymns, and its narrative character assured it from the outset a widespread reception. Even though it seems to have been written by Brahmins primarily for the *kṣatriya*, or warrior caste, its form and its implicit openness to the other castes meant it received a massive popular response from all levels of Indian society. This 'popular' aspect of the epic stimulated the emergence of numerous translations into the vernacular languages. That is how variations in the story appeared without, however, jeopardising the homogeneous nature of the whole. Faced with this proliferation, the need for the creation of a critical edition, taking into account the greatest number of manuscripts, was felt early on in Orientalist circles. A team of researchers, almost exclusively Indian, consequently embarked on this gigantic task from 1919, in Poona (today Pune) in Maharastra. The final text appeared in twenty-six volumes between 1933 and 1972. Unfortunately, it did not gain the unanimous acceptance of all scholars, who continue to refer to several different editions.

From the point of view of its form, the *Mahābhārata*, notwithstanding several short passages in prose, is essen-

---

aspects of the language of the epic. But the differences are minimal in relation to what is usually called classical Sanskrit.

11 Pāṇini does speak of a *Mahābhārata*, and he cites the names of Arjuna and Vāsudeva (Kṛṣṇa), but it is agreed that this can be seen as an allusion to some legends or to some cults that existed before the composing of the epic, properly so called.

tially composed in verse. It contains between ninety and a hundred thousand *śloka*, which makes it probably the longest narrative poem in the history of mankind. A *śloka* is a sort of short stanza containing two couplets, each one two times eight or two times eleven syllables. The Sanskrit metre obeys the same basic principles as the Greek and Latin ones, with alternate long and short syllables. If one considers that the translation of a *śloka* takes up about four lines in a prose translation, the whole epic would be, in a current edition with forty lines a page, a work of about ten thousand pages, approximately eight times the size of the *Iliad* and the *Odyssey* combined, or three and a half times that of the Bible! It should also be noted that the epic contains a late addendum of approximately ten thousand verses called the *Harivaṃśa*, *The Genealogy of Hari* (another name for Kṛṣṇa), which tells the story of the avatar's childhood.

As it has been transmitted to us, the *Mahābhārata* is a text which simultaneously deals with religion, politics, sociology, law, morality, cosmology, ritual, psychology and, last but not least, deliverance (*mokṣa*), which constitutes the ultimate goal of the human condition in the Hindu perspective. As an epic evocation of the birth of a nation it also satisfies a natural need, which all people feel, to know their ancestral origins. The form of ancestor worship that it establishes, equivalents of which we find in many other civilisations, only makes sense if, beyond the fathers of our fathers, we discover the truly divine origins of humanity, and this is why the principal protagonists of the *Mahābhārata* are, as we have said, all attached to the lunar dynasty of the god Candra. In these diverse ways, the epic has profoundly penetrated the Indian consciousness, whose social, intellectual and spiritual preoccupations it recapitulates in its own manner, and its influence has been considerable. Undoubtedly more than any other work in their immense cultural heritage, it has lived and lives on in the collective imagination of Indians whatever be their caste or belief. As a result it has provided all the arts with an abundance of themes. Poetry, literature, theatre, mime, dance, shadow plays and puppets, sculpture, painting and even, in our present time, comic strips and cinema have seized upon this inexhaustible fund to exploit it in a thousand ways, many giving it a regional stamp according to where these forms have been developed. But one must not forget that in India nothing can be separated from the sacred and the spirituality it transmits. And it is obvious that it is on the religious plane that the influence of the *Mahābhārata* has been the most considerable. The entire epic and, above all, its heart, the dialogue in the *Bhagavad-gītā* in which Kṛṣṇa overcomes Arjuna's despair and exhorts him to combat, is well and truly the origin of the religion of *bhakti*, devotion to a divine person in which the devotee meets God himself. Enriched by diverse sources, this religion would become what first the Muslims, arriving in India in the eighth century, and then the Europeans, called Hinduism. Although with the *Mahābhārata* we are, *a priori*, in the heart of the spiritual current called Vaisnavism to the extent that the epic recounts the deeds of Kṛṣṇa as an avatar of the god Viṣṇu, this exceptional work has nevertheless extended its influence into practically all the other spiritual currents of India.

2

The *Mahābhārata* as Seen Historically and in the West

IT WAS A SWISS MAN, Colonel Antoine-Louis de Polier of Lausanne, who, at the end of the eighteenth century, made the epic known for the first time to the Western world. While serving in the English East India Company, he became interested in the local traditions and brought back from his long stay there a pile of notes containing detailed summaries of the *Mahābhārata*, *Rāmāyaṇa* and *Bhāgavata-purāṇa*. His cousin, the canoness of Polier, arranged this material and some twenty years later (1809) brought out a book entitled *La Mythologie des Indous*, which fell into obscurity but which has been recently rehabilitated (see Dumézil 1968: 42–44, and Polier 1986). Since then several complete translations of the *Mahābhārata* have appeared, above all in English, and the epic has been the subject of innumerable studies by Orientalists. Thanks to Georges Dumézil and Madeleine Biardeau, France can boast of having two of the best experts on this subject.[1] Nevertheless, in an elegantly written pamphlet, *L'Oubli de l'Inde, Une amnésie philosophique* (2004), Roger-Pol Droit has mercilessly shown how the extraordinary work of French Indologists—and this well beyond a simple reference to works relating to the epic—has been and continues to be largely ignored by French philosophers, and unfortunately remains almost totally unknown to the general public.

Hindus never ask the question of whether the battle in the *Mahābhārata* really happened historically or not. They simply believe that it took place as the text recounts, notwithstanding the nature of its marvellous events. If things like that don't happen anymore, it is because the world has changed and hardened, and men no longer live on close terms as they did before with the gods and the supernatural. But the Indologists, no doubt from the beginning of their research, asked themselves if this story did not transmit the memory of an actual war. After having surveyed the literary Indian sources the great French Orientalist Louis Renou came to the conclusion that the *Mahābhārata* really was based on an historical event, the conflict between the Kuru and the Bhārata tribes already mentioned in the Vedic texts, even though all of this is difficult to date.[2] He says

---

1 To the names of these two authors should be added that of Alf Hiltebeitel of Chicago, whom we will have ample opportunity to cite later.

2 We are basing ourselves here on what he wrote in *L'Inde classique, manuel des études indiennes*, a collective work published under his direction and that of Jean Filliozat. This monument of erudition remains incontrovertible even if it was first published in 1947–49. In his preface to the 1985 edition, Pierre

> Concerning the Pāndava, one is forced to admit a historical basis. They are characters, blown up, amplified, what you will, whose authenticity is established by the facts, too many concrete details highlight this. The idea of a mythological *Mahābhārata* that is complacently believed by some appears untenable. The Great Quarrel could be situated at the end of the epoch of the *Ṛgveda*: the heroes of *Bhārata* are the immediate ancestors of king Janamejaya, son of Pariksit, which the later Vedic texts speak of as a contemporary and before whom it is said the epic was recited for the first time. (1985: 1,384).

Following on from Renou, a recent researcher has also suggested that the *Mahābhārata* is a legendary story based on two battles, that of the twenty kings and that of the ten kings, both mentioned in the *Ṛg-veda* (1, 53 and 7, 18).[3] But present day Indologists don't give much credence to these attempts to root the epic in historic soil. For one of the major difficulties in this thesis is the problem of the polyandrous marriage with Draupadī, the wife held in common by the five Pāṇḍava brothers. This would necessarily imply that the *kṣatriya* heroes of the poem were either of non-Aryan origin or that, at least, they had had to submit, in a domain so central socially as marriage, to an alien practice. Even

---

Filliozat, son of Jean, stresses again the irreplaceable nature of this work. Much time has passed since then, but the debates begun in this encyclopedia are still open.

3 Michael Witzel (1995), quoted by González-Reimann (2010: 18).

if one allows for the possibility that the source of such a contamination arose in India, which has, or at least had, several ethnic groups which traditionally practised polyandry, this is far from resolving the problem in question. But whatever the case may be, the presence of a possible historical 'trigger' remains anecdotal, especially in a country where a 'historic consciousness' similar to the Western one[4] does not exist. Even if a factual substratum is not incompatible with a mythological development, it is actually this development that gives the epic, if anything, its universality on the literary, symbolic and religious plane. Already the countless parallels that can be drawn between the *Mahābhārata* and the *Iliad* and the *Odyssey*—where historical events have also been sought[5]—has opened up, for a start, a much larger field of study for understanding the Indian epic. It is in their 'mythologisation' that historical events, if one wishes to refer to them, gain their full meaning in the genesis of a civilisation, and Christianity is no exception to this rule.

---

[4] This theme has been developed in *The Queen and the Avatar* (p. 46), stressing the fact that the Indian conception of history is linked to a perception of the world as *saṃsāra*, a continuous flux of impermanence.

[5] The amazing adventures of Heinrich Schliemann, whose efforts were richly rewarded by discovering the ruins of Troy, by no means imply that he had the final word on the interpretation of Homer's work. In addition the opinion of certain Orientalists who assert an influence of the *Iliad* in the composing of the *Mahābhārata*, inferred from Dio Chrysostom's mention of the existence of a translation of Homer's epic in India in the 1st century AD, cannot be rejected *a priori* even though it raises numerous problems.

In commenting on his belief in a never-ending elaboration and amplification of the basic historical kernel of the *Mahābhārata*, Renou does not fail to emphasise the tremendous diversity of material employed in the creation of the epic and the abundance of stylistic devices implemented. With its passages of prose, fables, legends, parables, speeches, genealogies, didactic and speculative sections, the *Mahābhārata* forms, in his eyes, a sort of popular encyclopaedia in that it addresses all the castes, which incidentally the language seems to confirm, written as it is in a relatively easy pan-Indian Sanskrit. The epic is, he concludes, 'The sum of Brahmanism, in which is found in all its luxuriant and formless grandeur, every aspect of the Indian genius' (*ibid.*, 1, 385). 'Formless'; the choice of this adjective illustrates, moreover, the difficulty Westerners have in feeling comfortable when deprived of their habitual categories, and we would have gladly replaced it with 'universal'!

Apart from the question of the actual historical origins of the *Mahābhārata*, Orientalists have obviously also posed the question of its date. On this point it is useless to consult the Hindus themselves. Their estimates fly in the face of all academic logic, for they put the writing of the epic in a dim and distant past which, when transposed into scientific chronology, does not add up to very much. For their part Western scholars remain divided into different camps over an important debate: should a work of this magnitude be attributed to only one author, or was it progressively elaborated on over the course of centuries with successive additions? We will return to this point later when we discuss the authorship of the work, but whatever the case may be, the range of time allowed for the writing of the epic is considerable—from the fourth century before to the fourth century after Jesus Christ! The least one can say is that a certain vagueness predominates. We will only mention here two Orientalist arguments of unequal worth which lead to the same conclusion in dating the writing of the epic to the beginning of this long period: the first one, belonging to Johannes Bronkhorst, provides an example of the kind of causality that modern criticism is capable of in such cases; the second is Madeleine Biardeau's, which has a certain credibility and is not incompatible with a traditional approach.

Johannes Bronkhorst sees in the *Mahābhārata* an attempt at conciliation between a Brahmanism defending its magical and spiritual prerogatives and the powers that be of the Maurya period (322–184) whose emperors showed a markedly 'heterodox' inclination towards local religions, such as Buddhism, Jainism and Ājīvikism. Established in India following the Aryan migrations, the Brahmins had at heart the plan of imposing their hierarchical conception of society, with themselves situated at the summit in their role as the keepers of the sacred Word and the authority of the *Veda*. 'Now in order to impose this vision, the Brahmins needed the support of the political powers, and in the first place, that of the kings' (2008: 49–51). According to Bronkhorst, the Brahmins were therefore not so much seeking to convert the populace as to exert power over the kings in order to safeguard their own supremacy. He adds,

> One of the ways adopted for imposing this vision of an ideal society and the manner in which

> it would be governed took shape in the two great epics of ancient India, the *Mahābhārata* and the *Rāmāyaṇa*. Both tell the story of just princes fighting unjust princes, and to do this they draw on older concepts that are not necessarily Brahmanic, but both have been reshaped in order to convey Brahmanic ideas on society (*ibid.*).

Among the non-Vedic ideas which seduced the Brahmins and were exploited by them, Bronkhorst especially cites the belief in rebirth and karmic retribution. However he concludes his argument by expressing a bizarre reservation, 'It is thus that the *Mahābhārata* constitutes a source of important yet complex information concerning Indian thought at this period, but too often its authors present a mixture of ideas which they have only very improperly understood'!

Starting from the same socio-religious premise, Madeleine Biardeau has developed a much more detailed argument. Her basic hypothesis is that the *Mahābhārata* represents '*une riposte*', as she says in French, by the Brahmanic tradition in the face of the growing importance assumed by Buddhism in India at the time of the emperor Aśoka,[6]

> ... the epic really intends to be a response to the enormous threat that the success of the Buddhist

[6] Aśoka, the famous emperor, was crowned in about 270–268 BC and he reigned for thirty-six years over an immense empire covering nearly the whole area of the traditional territory of India with the exception of the far South. His conversion to Buddhism is known by the countless stelae he erected everywhere.

> message and the insolence its royal protector posed to brahmanical society. It is Aśoka's empire, and not Buddhist literature, which started it all, by swamping the 'Middle Kingdom', home to Brahmanic orthodoxy according to Manu and to Krishnaite *bhakti* according to the epic.[7]

This hypothesis allows the author to logically and credibly set the date of the composing of the *Mahābhārata* towards the end of the 3rd and the beginning of the second century before our era. The war portrayed in the *Mahābhārata* becomes a reflection or metaphor for the crisis that Brahmanism was undergoing, faced with the expansion of Buddhism into its own territory. It should not be forgotten that in opening its teaching to all and in preaching a general renunciation of secular duties and a concomitant subordination of society to the community of monks, the Buddha shook the very foundations of the caste system and put it in great danger of breaking up altogether. The message of the *Mahābhārata* thus, most importantly, redefines *dharma*, particularly royal *dharma*,[8] since Aśoka's empire threatened the organisa-

[7] 2002: 1,128. Certain authors before Biardeau had already recognised Aśoka in the character of Duryodhana (Holtzmann, 1892–95), or more subtly in Dhṛtarāṣṭra (Simson, 1984, cited by Angelika Malinar, 2012: 75).

[8] The importance that Buddhism gives to this word is well known, even though it lends it a different meaning. To redefine *dharma* is also to readjust the concept to the Brahmanic context of the socioreligious ideology of the castes. Instead of producing a similar work to the *Mahābhārata* a thousand years later, Brahmanism made the caste system more rigid in response to the Muslim invasion.

tion of the temporal world of the Bhārata.[9] It marks the first step in the brahmanical reconquest of India through an urgent need to reassert the role of the *kṣatriya*, to whom fell naturally the task of leading society. The birth of the epic appeared then, in these circumstances, like a prelude to the total eradication of Buddhism in the peninsula, which we know would only be finally realised at a much later time with the Vedantic sage Śaṅkara (seventh century AD).

Madeleine Biardeau considers the *Mahābhārata* to be a sort of apocalypse born of a reaction to a state takeover of a new religion. In so doing, she is not unaware of the parallel to be found in the history of early Christianity.

> *Mutatis mutandis*, we are here in the Judaeo-Christian climate of the apocalypse and its fight against Greek cultural and Roman politico-religious aggression, when we witness the fierce defence of a Brahmanism whose most cherished beliefs were threatened by the attempt to belittle its socio-religious structure and revealed practices by the promise of the total impermanence of all being.[10]

---

9 Aśoka's role of unifying India, which was on the point of receiving the revelation of an avatar destined to impose his message on the whole country, is not without parallel to Caesar 'preparing', through his conquests and political function, for the slow spread of Christianity on a large scale within the Roman empire.

10 2002: 1, 160. From the point of view of the history of religions, one can always perceive the birth of a new religion as being the 'creation' or the 'invention' of the preceding religion whose limitations, whether formal, social or doctrinal, bring forth an

What the French scholar does not say is that, in the case of India, an ancient religion was reacting to a new one, whereas in the West it was the opposite case of a new religion defending itself from the last attacks of an ancient world.

For all that, the *Mahābhārata*, which would lead to a revitalisation of Brahmanic doctrines in the face of the Buddhist 'revolution', does not appear to be, in her thinking, a revelation according to the etymological sense of the word apocalypse. Rather, it stems from a sort of identity reflex which cannot be created *ex nihilo*.

> The Brahmin or Brahmins who created the poem ... more or less consciously used texts which had permeated their thinking since childhood like a normative language. For had they not, from a very early age on, spent their days in carefully memorising these texts by rote following methods which today leave us speechless, methods which ensured the transmission of the content rather than its comprehension? It is obvious that the texts thus interiorised acted like so many references or more simply, mental frameworks beyond which they were not able to think (1985: 1, 26–27).

This limitation, as described by the Indologist, in supposing that the authors of the *Mahābhārata* were able to draw on the Vedic sources only in a 'more or less' con-

---

eruption of the spirit opposed to the letter. Thus for some, Christianity appears as an invention of Judaism to the extent that the latter forced the disciples of Jesus to build their church beyond the Synagogue.

scious manner has, nevertheless, for us something rather ill-sounding about it in the same vein as the opinions of Bronkhorst quoted above. It seems to strangely belittle the value of the text in a way which is too trivial with regard to the challenge of the enterprise and the sublimity of the result. However, it should be mentioned that the Hindus also show a certain reserve with regard to the epic's degree of inspiration in placing it in the domain of *smṛti* (literally 'memory') and not of *śruti* (literally 'hearing'). This hierarchical division of religious literature appeared, it seems, for the first time in *The Laws of Manu*, the *Mānavadharmaśāstra* (2, 9–10), which dates from the beginning of the Christian era. It determines that only the Vedic texts, from the *Ṛg-veda* to the *Upaniṣad*, come from a direct revelation (*śruti*) received by the *ṛṣi*, the prophets or *uates*, listeners to the gods, and that subsequent writings come from a tradition (*smṛti*) transmitted by authors of a less lofty nature. The fact remains that the writings of a monumental literary work such as the *Mahābhārata* imply an authority which has nothing hazardous about it, and it is most significant that the *Bhagavad-gītā*, which forms an integral part of it, is generally agreed by Hindus to belong to the literature of *śruti*.

3

Vyāsa

THE CHARACTER Vyāsa, to whom tradition attributes the composition of the epic, presents an interesting analogy to Homer. The historic reality of these two authors is entirely conjectural, and both have names which primarily refer to their profession. Thus Homer, which means literally the Hostage, 'he who binds two belligerent parties by a pact,' plays the role, as creator of the *Iliad*, of 'Compiler' (of the Trojan story), at least if André Sauge's gloss (2000: 475) is to be believed. As for Vyāsa, his name signifies the Diffuser, which is obviously a title for his function. In contrast to the Greek *aoidós*, the Indian bard identifies himself with one of the principal protagonists of the epic, that is, Kṛṣṇa Dvaipāyana, or 'The Island-born' Kṛṣṇa, which gives him, in the opinion of Hindus, a pedigree and a distinct personality. It is precisely because he presents himself as the direct ancestor of both the Pāṇḍava and the Kaurava, and the eye-witness of the war which he survives, that he is able to retell the story and bequeath it to posterity. But besides this literary fiction, we do not know anything about him except that traditionally he is considered to be a compiler of the *Veda* and is rather generously attributed with the composition of the whole of the *Purāṇa*, whatever may be the supposed dates of the composition of the thirty-six works which make up this corpus. To which, further, and for good measure, is added a commentary on the philosophical works of Patañjali, the master of *Yoga*! It can be seen from all this that it is obviously here a matter of patronage. The question, as with Homer, of knowing whether there was only one author of the *Mahābhārata*, or if there was a chain of poets writing in succession over an undetermined period of time (which might have taken centuries) to compose the whole epic, remains debatable.

There is little doubt that a single authorship of the work is far from obvious to the vast majority of Orientalists, and Louis Renou, for example, after having examined a certain number of early data relating to its supposed genesis, or rather having (laboriously) reconstructed this genesis from the text, concludes, 'it follows on from this quite clearly that the *Mahābhārata* could not have been the work of only one man. The language, style and internal contradictions all bear witness to inequalities in its composition, confirmed in the artistic disparity between one part and another.' (1985: 1, 385). In support of this he imagines the slow elaboration of the epic over tens and even hundreds of years, which seems to be implied by its multiple Sanskrit recensions and vernacular versions. In the same vein Senart says: 'As it has come down to us, with its one hundred thousand verses full of disparities of all kinds, the Mahābhārata cannot possibly be considered the work of one man, or even of a whole generation' (1967: V). If Dumézil does not challenge the central premise of such a position,[1] Hiltebeitel (2001: 19ff.), paying closer attention to the unity of the work, comes up with the interesting hypothesis that the *ṛṣi* gathering together in Naimiṣa forest, like they do at the beginning of the *Mahābhārata* in the narrative framework of the epic, represent the community of authors who composed it and who thus portrayed themselves inside their own story. As a result he concludes that the overall work would have been composed in a relatively short space of time, in about twelve years, which is the exact time it took to complete the sacrifice, the *sattra*, performed at this gathering. He imagines that the sages with their varying skills would have worked under the direction of the master of this rite, namely Śaunaka, the Son of a Dog, who would have been its overall composer (*ibid.*, 169).

Madeleine Biardeau's position in this controversy is even more trenchant. She states

> ... its formal and semantic unity [referring to the *Mahābhārata*] on multiple levels of depth is such that it is impossible not to situate its creation at a very specific, short space of time, place and Brahmin milieu. At this point I can hear loud objections raised to this imaginary and anonymous creator of the MBh which goes against the received opinion of a slow, disorganised collective elaboration, but this is not the place to justify it. The refinement of construction and invention

[1] 'The question of the authorship of the poem does not arise: generations have contributed to the state in which we read it now' (1986[5]: 1, 34).

> that the Mbh shows can only be the work of a genius and I do not see what is to be gained by making him plural (1985: 1, 26–27).

It requires courage, based on an attentive study of the text and personal intuition, to take an opposing stand in this way to an academic position previously so ferociously defended.[2] That being said, Biardeau does not exclude the possibility that the author in question got help either from members of his family, as she imagines, or from others, which brings her in the end close to Hiltebeitel's point of view.

It remains for us to understand what is meant in this context by the quality of 'genius' attributed to this 'imaginary creator' by Madeleine Biardeau. This term has changed a lot since antiquity, when it meant the tutelary god of each individual (male), until its application today, a little indifferently and much inflated, to anyone showing innate intellectual and creative prowess which far surpasses the average man. In literature, we frequently confer this epithet on poets who, like Homer, Virgil, Dante and Shakespeare, have attained in the West the pinnacle of fame and have become in turn an inexhaustible source of inspiration. Vyāsa is without doubt cut from the same cloth, comparable above all, by force of circumstances, to the first named, even if certain purists

[2] It has been sometimes said that one whole life would not be enough for one author to create a work of this magnitude. Prolific writers are, however, not lacking in different literary domains. The personal diary of the Genevan H. F. Amiel, who also published a certain number of academic works, is composed of sixteen thousand pages—one and a half times the size of the *Mahābhārata*!

judge the style of the *Mahābhārata* to be much looser than the works of the authors on this ideal list. Naturally, a certain monotony and some tedious repetitions can be expected once one goes from a text of a few hundred pages to one comprising ten thousand.[3] But in spite of their immense influence on the arts, thought and culture of Western civilisation, and without counting that the canons of beauty differ necessarily from one civilisation to another, none of the writers cited above has played a role comparable to Vyāsa in the field of religion. In other words, for we are speaking of India here, none has similarly inspired whole peoples in their daily life and over such a very long period of time. This shows how inappropriate the word 'genius' is in this context, just as it would be if it were applied to one or another of the authors of the Torah or the Gospel.

Educated Hindus can, no doubt, conceive and accept that the *Mahābhārata* contains diverse borrowings, whether they be *ādivāsī*,[4] Dravidian or foreign, especially Greek. However, it is undeniable, in spite of different Sanskrit recensions and numerous vernacular versions, that the epic forms for them a coherent and perfect whole, and this coherence is undoubtedly linked to the epic's attribution, notwithstanding its immense size, to

---

3 A similar reproach about poverty of style has been equally but vainly launched at the Gospels, whose language, riddled with Semitisms, is notoriously different from the ancient language of classical Greek.

4 The *ādivāsī* are Indian aborigines who were present on the sub-continent before any invasion or migration. They represent today about 8 per cent of the country's population and are not Hindu at all.

one sole author whom we must now introduce. His name, Dvaipāyana, 'The Island-born',[5] contains an allusion to his origin. He was born, in fact, immediately he was conceived, of the clandestine union of Parāśara and Satyavatī, the daughter of the King of the Fish, on a boat hidden by a magical cloud in the middle of the Yamunā, and he spent the first part of his life on an island in that river. Like the great majority of principal heroes in the epic, he is the incarnation of a god. We will have occasion to return to this subject, which is of paramount importance. For the time being we will just say that he is a manifestation of Nārāyaṇa, that is to say Viṣṇu, the supreme god, as he is represented lying on a serpent in an ocean of milk, between two cosmic creations. His name, Kṛṣṇa, also indicates that he is a complementary aspect of Kṛṣṇa Vāsudeva, the central hero of the poem, but he is distinguished from his namesake by his caste, given that his father, Parāśara, is a Brahmin, in contrast to the avatar, Vāsudeva, who is a pure *kṣatriya*. The fact that his first three sons, that is, Dhṛtarāṣṭra, Pāṇḍu and Vidura, belong, by a strange chain of events, to the world of the *kṣatriya*, explains in its way the need, noted by Bronkhorst and others, for the Brahmins to deal with the representatives of temporal power whose hegemony had become too intrusive.[6]

---

5 The word is here translated according to Monier-Williams. Biardeau assimilates the island to a refuge and suggests '[He who is] made of those who go towards a refuge,' which despite its clumsiness, is also an acceptable interpretation.

6 Vyāsa was also the father, by a nymph, of a fourth son called Śuka, the Parrot, who would become his first disciple.

For the Hindus, Vyāsa is, what is more, a *ṛṣi*,[7] a seer or a prophet, which confers on him *de facto* the same dignity as that of the 'transmitters' of the hymns of the *Ṛg-veda*. As such he is said to have compiled and arranged all of these hymns. He is described as *brahmavādin*, bearer of the sacred word, and Vaiśampāyana, who will be discussed in the next chapter, says, 'Know that Kṛṣṇa Dvaipāyana Vyāsa is Nārāyaṇa, the Lord, because who other than the Lord could be the author of the *Mahābhārata*?' (12, 334, 9, quoted by Hiltebeitel 2001: 89). So it is not so much the length of the work as the source of inspiration which appears to be superhuman or supernatural in the minds of Indians.

Apart from the episode of his birth and his role in engendering the children of his half-brother Vicitravīrya with the latter's widows, Vyāsa appears more than once as an actor in his own story, of which traditionally he is the compiler. Thus Hiltebeitel counts at least forty-one appearances of the poet in the course of the epic (2001: 46ff.). He turns up from nowhere in order to guide his own characters with his advice or teachings. He carries all the authority conferred on him as a *ṛṣi* and he is revered by everyone. What is more, he is very often surrounded by a group of other famous *ṛṣi* when his heroes meet him during their trials. Then he disappears as mysteriously as he has come. In his way he incarnates, in his role as guide, the continuity between the Vedic tradition and the epic, from which he gets his common name, Vedavyāsa, the Diffuser of the *Veda*. In

[7] This word probably comes from the root *DṚŚ*, to see, found in the word *darśana*, vision, point of view.

many respects he is assumable, in his function as the demiurge in his work, to the god Brahmā, the Creator, even though nowhere is he presented as his incarnation. All the same, Hiltebeitel has an interesting hypothesis on this subject (2011: 110ff.). In noting that there are four characters having the name Kṛṣṇa, The Black, in the epic, he associates them with the four great gods of Hinduism, notably the three members of the *trimūrti* (Brahmā, Viṣṇu and Śiva) and the Devī. Vyāsa (Kṛṣṇa Dvaipāyana) is thus Brahmā, while Kṛṣṇa (Kṛṣṇa Vāsudeva, the son of Vasudeva) is Viṣṇu, whose avatar he is. Arjuna in turn represents Śiva.[8] Even though his name, *Arjuna*, means The Brilliant, The Silver One, he is also called Kṛṣṇa when he fights in the company of the avatar who drives his chariot. One speaks in this case of two Kṛṣṇa (*kṛṣṇau*, dual form). Finally, Draupadī, the daughter of Drupada, who is an incarnation of Śrī-Lakṣmī, the wife of Viṣṇu, has as a proper name Kṛṣṇā (with a feminine ending *-ā*) and corresponds in this play of associations to the Devī.

The adjective *kṛṣṇa* therefore means black, or rather blue-black,[9] and this colour is associated with the

---

[8] The Śaivite character of this formidable fighter is linked to his role as the 'destroyer' which he plays in the final battle where he uses a magic weapon that he got from the great god of the Himalaya.

[9] The difficulty experienced by philologists in translating words for colour from one language to another is well known. Latin has no word for the colour black, for instance. There is only *niger*, which describes a shiny black, and *ater* which is a matt black. The adjective *kṛṣṇa* refers to the night, which is dark blue, almost black, or to a cloud heavy with rain, and this is why in iconography Kṛṣṇa is painted blue.

kali-yuga, the last of the four ages inaugurated on the battlefield of Kurukṣetra. In another essay (where he only mentions Arjuna in passing), Hiltebeitel recalls that, according to the *Mahābhārata*, Kṛṣṇa appears in the previous ages in the colours white, red and yellow, in that order, before taking on the black colour in the last era. This range of colours indicates the successive predominance of the four *varṇa* (literally: colour), the four castes throughout the ages, that is, the *brāhmaṇa* (priests/white), the *kṣatriya* (warriors/red), the *vaiśya* (peasants, livestock-breeders, merchants, craftsmen/yellow) and the *śūdra* (servants/black).[10] It reflects the increasingly down-to-earth nature of the concerns of humanity and their growing opacity. In the same way, Vyāsa, as an incarnation of Nārāyaṇa, also appears in each age, and he only takes on a tenebrous form in the dark age (*kṛṣṇa-yuga*) when begetting Bharata's descendants, who are destined to fight against each other. As for Draupadī, she has, according to the *Vāmana-purāṇa*, also 'passed' successively through the colours white, red, yellow and blue (*nīla*), this last colour often being substituted for black and associated with the earth, which she also represents. The American scholar concludes, 'Thus, at the very least, the blackness of the three figures seems to be a sign of the times, that is, of the arrival or onset of the Kali yuga' (1990: 63). We will return later to the question of the four ages. For the moment we will just point out that these three characters share a com-

10 In another passage, the text reverses the red and yellow, perhaps with the intention of showing a gradual darkening, but red, the colour of blood, corresponds better to the warrior caste.

monality of colour and function that is very intimately linked to the god Viṣṇu, and this is borne out in more than one passage of the story. It is particularly transparent in a key episode where Vyāsa, Kṛṣṇa and Draupadī unite in their efforts to convince King Drupada to accept the polyandrous marriage of his daughter. In an entire chapter dedicated to this event (*ibid.*, ch. 3), Hiltebeitel demonstrates how this Vaisnavite 'clan' follows Śiva's plan of cyclical transformation which they cannot evade. What is more, in a previous life, Draupadī, who was anxious to get married, had prayed five times to the Himalayan god to give her a husband like Indra, thus opening the door to this infringement of the social order which would spark the war and lead to colossal upheavals in the world.

Vyāsa's divine origins and his identification with Nārāyaṇa are thus for Hindus concomitant with the embedding of the epic in the world of the gods. Tradition recounts, moreover, that Vyāsa produced his narrative under conditions that only increase the marvellous nature of the enterprise. It is said that he used the services of the god Gaṇeśa as secretary and that the god with the head of an elephant broke off one of his tusks to make a pen. A deal was made between the two partners. Vyāsa agreed to dictate his work in one go right till its completion, while Gaṇeśa would write nothing he had not fully understood. This is why at intervals Vyāsa dictated verses which were particularly difficult to understand, called *vyāsa-kūṭa*, in order to use the time it took Gaṇeśa to understand them to think of the next part of his story. That this lovely story is the product of a later interpolation, as many scholars believe, does not detract from its value on the traditional plane, but it may also reveal that the story was put into writing only after a more or less lengthy, uniquely oral, transmission.

4

The *Mahābhārata* and the *Iliad*

WE HAVE JUST seen in the last chapter that the character Vyāsa is somewhat analogous to Homer, and it is undeniable that the *Mahābhārata* immediately calls to mind, for the Western reader, the *Iliad*, the founding text of European literature. The relationship between these two works derives from their common Indo-European origins, a subject that will be discussed in the next chapter. For now we will limit ourselves to some general observations. Through their primacy and their role as masterpieces these two unrivalled texts have become, since the time of their creation, powerful models in their respective cultures. In addition, the Greek epic, like its Indian equivalent, also refers back to a mythical war whose historical substratum, if ever it had one, is vague, if not irrelevant. We are placed on a world stage, in the middle of a human melee where heroes incarnating gods clash. Even if in the *Mahābhārata*, as in Greece, the clan that seems to be the most righteous eventually wins, one cannot turn the Kurukṣetra war into a simplistic fight between 'good and evil', as is sometimes made out. One readily simplifies the *Mahābhārata* in reducing it to a metaphorical struggle waging for all eternity between the *deva* and the *asura*, the gods and the demons, or as Coomaraswamy renders them, the Angels and the Titans. While this interpretation is certainly not to be rejected, and is, what is more, perfectly justified in numerous explicit passages in the epic itself, it should not delude us as to the complex state of reality found on the 'bad' side, where there are heroes or characters who eminently represent chivalric and therefore spiritual values which are in no way inferior to those shown by their staunchest enemies. In the Kaurava army, for example, neither the venerable Bhīṣma nor the master of arms, Droṇa, are in any way demonic. Equally, in the *Iliad* Hector is the picture of chivalry, and it is the same with Aeneas, whom Virgil portrays as an incomparable hero who is the ancestor of the founding father of Rome.[1] What is more, the presence in the *Mahābhārata* of a character representing *dharma*, cosmic order, in both camps—that is, Yudhiṣṭhira with the Pāṇḍava, and Vidura with the Kaurava—demonstrates the simplistic nature of such a generalisation. It has been suggested more than once in this regard that in the polytheistic[2] climate, where there are unlimited numbers of gods to personify the forces at work in the world, the tortuous problem of good and evil is, as a natural consequence, completely avoided. And

[1] The kings of France, amongst others, boast of Trojan ancestry.

[2] It is obvious that this word should be taken in a provisional and relative sense. There is no religion where the idea of unicity does not appear in one way or another: in India it is evident in the concept of *brahman*, and in Greece it is found in the majority of the philosophical schools.

this lack of concern is not without relevance to the morality of the civilisations which have such a perspective.

It is not our intention to set out a detailed comparison between the *Iliad* and the *Mahābhārata* in this chapter, which would demand a thorough study taking into account both the similarities and the differences. But we think it important that the reader keeps in mind a few of the main elements common to the two epics in order to fully appreciate what comes later, for it seems hopelessly limiting to begin a reading of Indian works as if they belonged to a world totally foreign to ours. Thus, it should be mentioned that in Greece as well as in India it is a woman who symbolises, in the last analysis, the cause of the conflict, despite the differing scenarios. While the Greeks will not give up until they get Helen back, unjustly stolen in their eyes by Paris, Duryodhana does not consider his victory complete until he has seized Draupadī, wife of the Pāṇḍava, in order to humiliate her and them completely. In both cases however, *dharma* demands that the marriage contract not be violated.

It is, in addition, by a ruse, which is not altogether devoid of treachery, that both Ulysses and Kṛṣṇa gain victory for their respective clans. Laocoon's cry to his countrymen duped by the wooden horse of the Greeks, *sic notus Ulixes?* 'So you think you know Ulysses?' would be echoed throughout Europe thereafter in a tenacious suspicion of the Greeks and a certain doubt cast on the use of the intelligence during the Christian Middle Ages. What is striking, in any case, is that in Greece as well as India, the epic introduced a conditional justification for deceit in the context of legitimate self-defence. We will return to this important question later (cf. ch. 12).

There is, moreover, another major point of convergence between the Trojan War and that of the *Mahābhārata*. The two conflicts take place at a precise moment in the history of the world and reflect specific spiritual concerns. India and Greece are perfectly united in this respect, teaching that mankind passes through successive periods characterised by a deterioration of human values and living conditions, causing widespread war in its final phase. This is the doctrine of the four ages associated by the Greeks with increasingly base metals, starting with gold, then silver, bronze and finally iron, and which, aside from this symbolism of metals, has its exact equivalent in India, as we shall see later on. Even if India places this cycle in a much broader vision than Greece, in multiplying the repetition of cycles to infinity, the two perspectives agree perfectly on the essential, by both placing present day man, the direct heir of this pivotal epoch, in a situation of extreme urgency demanding a rethinking of all the norms of behaviour. It should nevertheless be noted that there is a slight difference in the traditional dating of these epics. Whereas the war in the *Mahābhārata* takes place at exactly the time of transition between the third and the fourth age, the *dvāpara-yuga* and the *kali-yuga*, the Trojan War seems to take place a little later, at least according to Hesiod's *Works and Days*, which introduces a sort of subdivision within the fourth age that does not exist in India and which he names the Age of Heroes. This means that the cyclic upheaval which starts the Trojan War in the Greek tradition must be placed at an indeterminate moment in the first part of the Iron Age, but not at its beginning. In spite of this difference, the two epic conflicts, both Indian and Greek, share the same function of being an intermediate stage between the mythic and historical eras.

Just like the *Iliad* in Greece, the *Mahābhārata* is India's oldest lengthy narrative giving rise to a mythology where the gods, or rather the heroes who descend from them in various ways, are put centre stage, and enter concretely into the framework of a narrative fiction which humanises them, at least up to a certain point. The birth of a literary genre necessarily reflects the concerns of the period in which it develops. It reveals the intimate needs of the people living then. The appearance of the autobiography at the time of Saint Augustine, the novel with Chrétien de Troyes and others, or again, in a lesser genre, the detective story with Edgar Allan Poe, should be considered in this light. We will return to this question when we examine the way in which India traditionally perceives the imagery of the epic. We will restrict ourselves at the moment, however, to two remarks. Firstly, it is interesting to note that it is not altogether unusual for the same literary genre, or at least closely related genres, to appear together at about the same time in different civilisations without any discernible mutual influence, as if this type of evolution was so to speak in the air at the time. In relation to the Greek and Sanskrit epics that concern us here, one could imagine, as others have, that the *Iliad* had an influence on the *Mahābhārata* or its composers, and it is certainly true that Greece and India have a common Indo-European heritage, but that does not explain how and why these twin works gained a central importance which was so sudden and so considerable in two such autonomous and independently developing worlds. In fact, only astrology can offer an answer to this difficulty, for it is the only science which writes history in a rhythmic and symbolic way, embracing in its perspective all of humanity, independently of the watertight compartments which separate the different peoples of the world from each other. Certainly anything and everything has been said on this subject. But one must be careful not to throw the baby out with the bath water. Secondly, in Greece it is symptomatic that this birth of the epic did not come without a certain gritting of teeth and resistance. The criticisms of Plato with regard to Homer, whom he banished from his Republic, are well known (*The Republic*, 606e–608b). And Hieronymus, for example, recounts that Pythagoras on descending into hell saw the soul of Hesiod attached to a column of bronze and screaming. As for Homer's soul, it was hung from a tree surrounded by snakes. He learnt that all these afflictions occurred to them because of all the stories they had made up about the gods (Diogenes Laertius, 8, 1). As for Xenophon of Colophon (end of the fourth century BC), he says, 'Homer and Hesiod attributed to the gods all things which are disreputable and worthy of blame when done by men; and they told of them many lawless deeds, stealing, adultery and deception of each other' (Fr. 7, Arthur Fairbanks). It could be imagined that the *Mahābhārata* also provoked a stir in certain Brahmin circles. However, to our knowledge there is altogether no trace of this reaction, and in a certain sense India succeeded where Greece failed, in uniting religion and mythology so effectively and permanently together.

5

The Birth of a Mythology

THE *MAHĀBHĀRATA* belongs to a group of writings which, like the Bible and the Qur'an, established a religion and laid the foundations of a civilisation. We mean by this that the epic explicitly guides[1] the devotees whom it addresses in three ways: first, it teaches them a doctrine in explaining the mysterious ways of the gods in the world, and in specifying their role in relation to its evolution or, rather, degeneration; next, it defines a morality and reminds men of the function of the castes and the duties, the *svadharma*, attached to them, and describes innumerable patterns of behaviour which should be either followed or avoided; finally, it exalts and preaches a new spiritual attitude, *bhakti-yoga*, the way of devotion, which replaces the vedic-sacrifice (*yajña*) with personal worship known as *pūjā*. It is not at all surprising that the passage from myth to epic, or from myth to mythology, brings with it upheavals

[1] This concrete guidance is given above all in the *Bhagavad-gītā*, to which we have dedicated a whole chapter. In this way of seeing things, the whole *Mahābhārata* appears as an immense illustration of the teachings of the *Gītā*.

of a religious nature, for men change with time, and therefore have need of new supports for their spiritual realisation. The shift from one age to another involves a change in mentality, and this change explains in its turn the emergence of a new literary genre in the sacred scriptures. This is why, in the Hindu consciousness, the Vedic literature—at least in its oldest elliptical and difficult to interpret form—appears as a relic of a bygone age, that of the third age, the *dvāpara-yuga*, the equivalent of the bronze age in the Greek tradition. This is not to say that this literature has lost all its authority, relevance and efficacy: far from it, for it continues to enjoy an unrivalled prestige, and certain Vedic, especially domestic, rites are practised to this day by Brahmins. But certainly it was at this point that the Vedic tradition gave way to new scriptural forms. In the same way, in the Christian consciousness, the New Testament appears as a rereading of the Old Testament and has largely replaced it in the practices and meditations of today.

In his retrospective vision of the history of mankind, René Guénon saw 'barriers' preventing contemporary man, unless endowed with a rare spiritual intuition, from really knowing and understanding what had happened before his own time (2001: 128–136). The greatest of these barriers was for him the sixth century BC. This corresponds to the beginning of history properly so-called, so much so that it is often defined as the era directly following the widespread use of writing in the transmission of knowledge. The very concept of history or of 'enquiry'—for that is the etymological meaning of the word—dates from Herodotus, and it is most significant in this context that the Buddha, the first undoubtedly historical person included in Vaisnavite mythology and who, as Biardeau has shown, seems to have played an important role in the emergence of the latter, was practically a contemporary of the Greek writer. That said, the case of India presents a triple particularity. First of all, contrary to what took place in the West, the *sanātana-dharma*[2] preserved with the Vedic corpus a great mass of writings from a past which, almost everywhere else in the world, corresponds to the prehistoric era, in the relative sense described above. Next, one seeks in vain, in the ideology and imagination of Indian civilisation as it developed after the epic appeared, for an equivalent of the historical consciousness that has so marked European thought. Lastly, the tradition of the *sanātana-dharma* offers the faithful a spiritual and existential perspective which dates back to a time before the birth of history, and which Guénon places at the beginning of the *kali-yuga*, that is, at about 4000 BC.[3] *Smṛti*, the collective memory, continued to be nourished on myths and very archaic concepts, even if it seems evident that a clear understanding of the ancient texts, starting with the *Ṛg-veda*, eluded the majority of Brahmins. Nevertheless, in plunging its roots deep

---

2 That is to say, the perennial religion or order. This is what Indians call their own tradition, making no distinction between Vedism, Brahmanism and Hinduism. These denominations created by Orientalists are of incontestable interest in the analysis of the evolution of the different beliefs in India, but one must not lose sight of the sentiment of perennial continuity present in the way that those who live this tradition perceive it.

3 We will examine his thesis on this dating in detail further on in the chapter on the four ages.

in that ancient and prodigious corpus of writings, the *Mahābhārata*, while fulfilling its role of adaptation and renewal, appears as a sort of direct testament to, or legacy of, the third age within the historical period.

The literary genre called *itihāsa* described above (ch. 1), which the *Purāṇa* took over, thus introduced and disseminated a mythology, as we understand the current use of the term, for example, in the phrase 'Greek mythology'. To really grasp what happened—to the extent we can attempt to explain it—it should be understood that in the Vedic period the gods seemed to only have a 'theological' personality. By this we mean that the *Veda*, which make up a collection of hymns, whether to accompany a given sacrifice or not, teach us basically about the different functions of the gods, their respective roles in the pantheon, and the special favours they can give when necessary, but they do not as yet share with us their 'lives' and all their 'doings' in detail, as would happen later in the *Purāṇa*. Certainly there existed at an earlier epoch myths which concerned them, and the oldest texts make constant allusion to them. But whether these myths were only transmitted orally or whether the texts that mention them have been lost, we can only imagine or reconstruct them in an incomplete fashion.[4] It is only in the subsequent literature immediately following the Vedic hymns that one can find a significant number of stories about the gods. We are referring to the *Brāhmaṇa*

---

4 This gap should not imply a 'secondary' or 'peripheral' character to the mythology in the Vedic religion. It shows, however, that in this civilisation which possessed the skills necessary for a strong oral tradition, this aspect of sacred knowledge was clearly of less importance.

and the *Āraṇyaka* (two categories of text still belonging to *śruti*) whose composition is prior to the emergence of Buddhism. Now, this sort of addenda to the hymns significantly complemented the overall picture of the Vedic pantheon that is the basis of the *Mahābhārata*, which used this source by transposing it in an original way. Danielle Feller (2004) has dedicated an important study to this aspect of the epic in examining the myths of the dissimulation of Agni, the seduction of Ahalyā by Indra, the stealing of Soma, and the story of Upamanyu saved by the Aśvin. She has thus found a subtle 'echo' of these myths—the expression and quotation marks are hers—in the epic story. Similarly, to give another example, Hiltebeitel has established an interesting parallel between the tenth book of the *Mahābhārata*, the *Sauptikaparvan*, which recounts the vengeful mission of Rudra under the guise of Aśvatthāman, and the myth of the destruction of the rite of Dakṣa by Śiva (1990: 312–335).

The fact remains, however, that these mythical episodes are far from playing a central role in the general framework of the epic, notwithstanding the relevance and usefulness of their inclusion. All of this must not let us lose sight of the fact that in the last analysis the epic has a new intention and, in intimately involving the old gods on the world stage, the *Mahābhārata* does something truly 'revolutionary'. We have shown in our introduction to *The Queen and the Avatar* what the main consequences of this radical change were: having appeared among men, the gods proved to be representable and, to use a phrase coined by Angot (2001: 132), worship became iconic. This completely new veneration of images, *pūjā*, is thus fundamentally linked to *bhakti* and the epic. Besides the religious upheaval that this entailed, its social impact should not be underestimated. In spite of some interpretations, the epic is aimed at a much wider audience than the *kṣatriya*, and it has incontestably enhanced the prestige of the lower castes. This is evidenced by the development, among other things, of the arts, which have enlisted the representatives of a host of diverse crafts, be it for temple construction or the creation of statues.

It was stated above that the ancient gods intervened in world history in incarnating, partially or wholly, as the characters in the *Mahābhārata*. In fact, practically all the important figures in the epic are either the sons or daughters of Vedic gods, be they the direct incarnations of these or new manifestations of *asura*, demons, already mentioned in the *Brāhmaṇa*. We have already discussed Vyāsa and Kṛṣṇa and their common relationship to Nārāyaṇa. We will now take the central example of the Pāṇḍava, the putative sons of Pāṇḍu, who was incapable of procreating directly because of the curse which he lived under. His first wife Kuntī's three sons, Yudhiṣṭhira, Bhīma and Arjuna, respectively, were born thanks to the intervention of the gods Dharma,[5] Vāyu and Indra. As

[5] In contrast to the other gods on this list, Dharma is not a Vedic god in the strict sense. But according to Dumézil, he synthesises the virtues associated with the gods Mitra and Varuṇa, who are most of the time spoken of together. We will see in chapter 11, especially dedicated to Yudhiṣṭhira, that neither Coomaraswamy nor Hiltebeitel, for different reasons, agree with Dumézil on this point. That said, it should be added that these two gods incarnate the basic contract between God and man. Mitra represents the 'gentle' side and Varuṇa the 'severe' side, for it involves a contract that cannot be broken

for his second wife Mādrī's twins, Nakula and Sahadeva, they were born due to the intervention of the Aśvin. Bhīṣma is an incarnation of Dyu, the Sky; Droṇa is Bṛhaspati, the priest of the gods; Vidura is a second Dharma, and so on. We will not provide here a complete list of the correspondences, as that would be tedious. They will only be mentioned when they come up, and the reader can also refer to the glossary where the pedigree of all the heroes is given.

The majority of the early Orientalists thought the link in kinship uniting the epic's heroes to the Vedic gods was a later addition. It took Georges Dumézil, carrying on from the work of Stig Wikander, to set the record straight. Methodologically, from the outset, the great French scholar of comparative studies took a different stand from Renou's, and in relation to the latter's statement that the idea of a mythical *Mahābhārata* was untenable (cf. ch. 2), he declared his interpretation to be the opposite of his predecessor's (1986^5: 33).[6] His field of research was comparative mythology, specifically of the Indo-European peoples. Drawing on his breathtaking erudition, he posited, within the framework of the

---

without serious consequences. But despite his severity, Varuṇa is always depicted in the *Veda* as a fundamentally benevolent god. These traits can be recognised in the polarity expressed in the Abrahamic religions in the terms concerning the love of God and the fear of God, or mercy and rigour.

6 Dumézil's most important work concerning these questions is his monumental *Myth and Epic*, which has been constantly in print and which comprises three volumes of about 1500 pages (cf. bibliography). The first 250 pages of the first volume are nearly exclusively on the *Mahābhārata*.

epic, the idea of a tripartite division in the function and hierarchy of society, comprising magical and legal sovereignty, physical strength and fertility. The guardians of the sacred, the priests, assume the first role in defining the perennial values of maintaining the social order and its ordering in relation to man's final ends. The kings and warriors, in their protective role, secure for the community its effective independence and the peace necessary for the harmonious running of earthly life. Finally, the farmers, raisers of livestock, craftsmen and traders, are responsible for the material well-being of society by providing the food and objects necessary to its existence.[7] We will see further on how the Pāṇḍava incarnate, through their divine affiliations, the various aspects of these three functions.

It is the Indian, Iranian, Roman, Greek, Scandinavian, Irish and Caucasian (Ossetian) traditions which Dumézil mainly focuses on, and who on surveying the findings of his research, concluded that, 'From a comparison of all the important texts [...] it is clear that it was the two Indo-Iranian and Roman societies which drew on the broadest epic and historical elements of the tripartite function' (*ibid.*, 632). The inclusion of India is somewhat obvious in this context to the extent that the caste system is a particularly explicit development of the trifunctional thesis.[8] As for Rome, its importance

---

[7] This last category occupies a privileged position with Dumézil due to its complex and multifaceted nature.

[8] It refers here to *varṇa*, the socio-religious division of Indian society and not to *jāti*, the socio-professional division. The *varṇa* are traditionally numbered at 4, but it is of course the first three, the Brahmins (priests), the *kṣatriya* (warriors) and

in this debate derives more from what is known or can be reconstructed of its early period than from the importation, which came relatively late, of elements that it took from Greek mythology. This importation was limited to the artistic and literary domain and did not affect the religious institutions at all. Although far from neglecting the works of Propertius or Virgil (primarily, with regard to the latter, the second half of the *Aeneid*), Dumézil applied himself above all to dissecting the first books of Livy. And it was to the extent that the Latin writer gave a historical appearance or coloration to very ancient myths, as if to sanction their validity,[9] that in the above quote Dumézil could speak of 'historical elements of the tripartite function'.

It has often been objected that Dumézil's theory of the three functions is not specifically Indo-European at all and that all societies, one way and another, can demonstrate that they have, at the least, the equivalent structures. His defence is clear, 'The answer [to this

---

the *vaiśya* (farmers, breeders, merchants and craftsmen) that interest Dumézil. The fourth *varṇa* is that of the *śūdra* (servants) who are subordinate to the former groups. Nevertheless, this clear fourfold partition of society raises a valid objection to Dumézil's theory. As Madeleine Biardeau has said regarding this: 'Indian society has never been trifunctional. A society hypnotised by the idea of the pure and impure cannot live without a section of society dedicated to impure functions' (2002: 1, 35).

9 In the same way, Christianity has always affirmed that the divine incarnation of Jesus, in addition to its eminently mythical value, derives its truth and its spiritual efficacy from the fact that it is a historical event and therefore absolutely 'real'.

objection] is not in doubt. While all three functions correspond to three needs of any society which must be satisfied if it is not to perish, there are very few peoples who have drawn an explicit or implicit ideology from this natural structure' (*ibid.*, 632). We cannot in the space of this short book relate all of Dumézil's arguments in proof of this theory, so we will limit ourselves to pointing out a few salient features that will complement and enrich subsequent developments dedicated to the traditional approach to the epic.

It therefore appears to Dumézil, that Dharma (Mitra-Varuṇa) eminently represents the sacerdotal function, Vāyu and Indra, the warrior function, and the Aśvin, the nurturing function. The doubling up in the epic of the second and third functions, highlighted by comparisons with other Indo-European mythologies, can be briefly summarised in the polarity Strength-Speed for the warrior function and Beauty-Intelligence for the nurturing function. This is why Bhīma, the son of the Wind, is constantly described as colossally strong, whereas it is Arjuna's skill with the bow which is his essential characteristic. In the same way it is his beauty which is Nakula's salient trait, whereas Sahadeva is distinguished by his intelligence and technical skill. The cardinal virtues of the representatives of the three functions are found synthesised in the respective notions of *dharma* (order, justice and rectitude),[10] *bala* (force) and *rūpa* (beauty). The split between the first two functions (corresponding to the di-

10 The word *dharma* comes from the root *DHṚ*, to carry, bear. This word is the exact etymological equivalent via the Indo-European, of the Latin *firmus*, which gives to English the adjective *firm* (the consonant *dh* in Sanskrit frequently

vision between spiritual authority and temporal power), on the one hand, and the third, which does not participate directly in the government of society, on the other, is illustrated by the fact that the first three Pāṇḍava have the same mother, the pious and enterprising Kuntī, and the last two have the beautiful Mādrī. The qualities that the author of the epic attributes to these two women thus correspond to the functions of their respective sons.

It can be seen now more clearly from this what the role of Draupadī, the common wife of the five brothers,[11] is; for the quintuple marriage—an abnormality amongst the Aryans and not very likely, as we have seen above, to be the result of an ethnic trait which had crept in—demands *de facto* a symbolical interpretation. The brotherhood of the Pāṇḍava, whose harmony is constantly stressed in the text, except for the odd moderate 'falling out', represents the state of the ideal society. Now, Draupadī, as the incarnation of Śrī, Prosperity, specifically manifests this harmony by ensuring its durability. Śrī is none other than the divine wife of Viṣṇu, but in becoming Draupadī in the *Mahābhārata*, she acquires a more complex personality.[12] It is said, in fact, that the

---

corresponds to the *f* in Latin). *Dharma*, the law, the perennial order, is what 'holds up' the world.

[11] With regard to this it should be said that Bhīma and Arjuna marry or have relations with several women, whereas their three brothers remain monogamous. Polygamy therefore seems to be, in this context, a privilege of the second function.

[12] Dumézil is at pains to explain why, as Śrī (or Lakṣmī, The Millionaire, The Fortunate), in other words, as the consort of Viṣṇu, Draupadī is not the wife of Kṛṣṇa, who incarnates Viṣṇu in the epic: 'There is a discrepancy here which the

daughter of King Drupada was born with a twin brother, Dhṛṣṭadyumna, the future general-in-chief of the Pāṇḍava army, directly from a sacrificial fire. Her true father is therefore the god Agni, Fire, and significantly she has no other mother than the sacrificial altar, the *vedī*, which symbolises the Earth. As the daughter of Agni, she inevitably incarnates *śakti*, the actualising power or energy, and as such her presence at the side of the five brothers is completely justified. As Dumézil says: 'Among the individual [Vedic] male gods, Agni is clearly the only one who is constantly trifunctional' (*ibid.*, 1, 119). Draupadī's importance as a symbol of the Earth, on the contrary, initially escaped the French scholar, who nevertheless admitted his mistake in a subsequent note ten years after the first edition of *Myth and Epic* (*ibid.*, 1, 639). For, from the moment the polyandrous heroine embodies the ultimate stake in the dice game which pits Duryodhana against Yudhiṣṭhira, she 'naturally' represents the prosperity linked to the possession of the kingdom and thus to the Earth. The sexual undertones of the scene when the Kaurava slaps his thigh to show that she is now his undoubtedly reinforce this interpretation.

Dumézil examines at length another very important aspect of this polyandrous marriage. It is a question, found elsewhere in the *Mahābhārata* (1, 197, 7275–7318), of a legend in which Draupadī is made the wife of a

---

Western mind can easily turn into bedroom farce, as Viṣṇu is well and truly incarnate in another hero of the poem, Kṛṣṇa, and that the meetings between Kṛṣṇa, Draupadī and her five husbands happen very often' (*ibid.*, 1, 118). We have suggested an explanation to this difficulty in *The Queen and the Avatar* (p. 129) and we will return to this later (ch. 9).

quintuple manifestation of the god Indra, incarnated simultaneously among the five brothers. This episode has the advantage of restoring Arjuna to his rightful place in this marriage, since he is the only direct son of Indra, who had won Drupada's daughter and who should have kept her for himself. We know that the five brothers were compelled to marry her communally because of the irrevocable injunction of Kuntī, who, not knowing that the prize won in the competition by her third son was a woman, told him to share his winnings with his brothers. This *felix culpa*, her unexpected pronouncement, becomes in the story the subject of a debate between the father and brother of Draupadī, who are really offended by the apparently scandalous nature of the polyandrous marriage, and the Pāṇḍava brothers who do not dare oppose their mother's wishes. They resort to the judgement of Kṛṣṇa and the sage Vyāsa, who decide in the way we have already seen, while reassuring everybody of the auspicious nature of this union.

We will not go into further detail now concerning Dumézil's analyses, and will simply refer the interested reader to his *Myth and Epic*, which is relatively easy to read despite the complexity of the subject and the abundance of data drawn from countless sources. We will only note that in his copious documenting of the epic heritage of the trifunctional theory, he definitively proved that the *Mahābhārata* has undeniable Indo-European roots. He also proved that comparative mythology can furnish a significant number of keys to it. Let him then conclude with regard to this:

> The Mahābhārata is, in essence, the transposition to the world of men, of a vast system of mythical images: the principal gods, surrounding the gods denoting the three functions, and some demons, are not just at close quarters to the main heroes but are their models and the conceptual relationships between these gods are translated in the heroes in terms of their kinship (brothers, wife) or friendly and hostile alliances. The plot of the poem is the transposition of a myth relating to a massive world crisis; the clash between the forces of good and evil grows until its destructive climax gives rise to a rebirth (*ibid.*, 1, 238).

But beyond this valuable contribution, Dumézil leaves the field open to other interpretations, scholarly as well as traditional, which will now be our main focus. Besides, the mention of good and evil poses a problem. These concepts are far too Western to account for the difference between *dharma* and *adharma*. What is more, the eroding power of Śiva, whose continual, underlying acts of world transformation go against the current of Viṣṇu and his work of preservation, are not in any way comparable to the evil of the Christian tradition. It is significant that Dumézil had very little to say about the role of Kṛṣṇa, who, in many respects is, nevertheless, one of the most important characters in the poem, and this it seems for the simple reason that he does not play an important role within the trifunctional structure.[13] In truth, only the Hindu tradition properly so called is able

[13] 'Despite his importance, Kṛṣṇa will not detain us long. He is straightforward' (*ibid.*, 1, 210). —Yes and no!

to fully teach us about the true function of the avatar, as we shall see.

6

The Primordial Forest

UNTIL NOW we have only briefly alluded to the *Mahābhārata's* story framework: it is time to return to this. In the first book of the epic we are introduced to a scene in a forest whose location is uncertain but where a company of *ṛṣi* have gathered for an important sacrificial rite. Among them unexpectedly appears a *sūta*, a charioteer, named Ugraśravas, 'He who has heard (or tells of) terrible things.' According to tradition it was the custom for minstrels to perform during the pauses in between the sacrificial rites, and the *sūta* who, on their chariots, used to proclaim the great deeds of the warriors they drove into battle, naturally took on the role of heralds or bards. Now, Ugraśravas has a marvellous story to tell. He has just come from attending a sacrifice held by King Janamejaya to avenge the death of his father who had been killed by a snake. Janamejaya is none other than the son of Parikṣit, Yudhiṣṭhira's great nephew and the successor to the throne of the kingdom of the Bhārata. On that occasion another *sūta*, Vaiśampāyana, who was Vyāsa's disciple, had told the king the whole story of the war of Kurukṣetra as it had been narrated to him by his own master. This is how Ugraśravas, at the request of the assembly of *ṛṣi* gathered in the forest, is invited, in turn, to recount this fabulous story just as he had heard it told from the mouth of Vaiśampāyana. This literary device is in itself simple and rather hackneyed, even if it appears quite sophisticated in the present case: the author introduces a narrator who, for want of witnessing the events himself, quotes the son of one of the main protagonists in the plot! The whole scene is bathed in a truly Vedic atmosphere, and we undoubtedly see here, reflected in a scene within a scene, the birth of the epic in the fertile earth of the earlier tradition in which it is so firmly rooted.

Conducted by the Brahmins on behalf of the sacrificant who paid for the costs, sacrifice (*yajña*) is the most essential act, or rite, of the Vedic religion. It always takes place in the open air on a temporary site consecrated for this purpose. It has many forms and its intention can be very varied. The accomplishment of the sacrifice creates a link between man and the gods whom he addresses. The gods are invoked in order to obtain some benefit such as prosperity, health, long life, riches in cattle and male descendants, etc., but never as an act of thanksgiving (Renou 1985: 1, 345). In doing so, one sanctifies the profane world by offering a victim which is thereby redeemed itself. The Vedic roots of the *Mahābhārata* are particularly noticeable in the sacrificial dimension that the Kurukṣetra war takes on and which, in many respects, appears as an epic and mythological transposition of the Vedic sacrifice, as far as it can be reconstructed from the most ancient texts and the ritual practices maintained right up to the present day. This rootedness has been perfectly well understood and analysed by recent Indologists, as well as the gap (*l'écart*: *sic* Biardeau) that has opened up between the epic and its model. This gap is most marked in the emergence of two gods who play only a secondary or minor role in the Vedic hymns, and yet who have now become the central figures of Hinduism. These two gods are Viṣṇu and Śiva (Rudra):

> It is impossible today not to see immediately the pivotal role these two divinities played in the sacrifice, as the poles of the sacrificial area: Rudra and his deadly fire needed to convey the nourishing odour to the gods, Viṣṇu, the creator of the sacrificial and, beyond it, cosmic, space and his fertilising link to the sacrificial stake. As such they preside over the sacrificial rite, and it is on the basis of this rite and its many aspects that they were transformed into the supreme gods of Brahmanism, while keeping their own identities even in the negation of this rite (2002: 1, 129).

The *Ṛg-veda* (7,99; 8, 29; 8, 52) actually speaks of the three gigantic steps made by Viṣṇu to open the sacrificial site to the gods and pave the way for the exploits of Indra. This myth will be taken up again later in the mythology of his incarnation as the dwarf Vāmana, the fifth major avatar, which makes of him a god of space who measures the world even as he measured the sacrificial site.[1]

---

[1] Hiltebeitel (1990: ch. 6) judiciously associates the three steps of Viṣṇu, as Vāmana, to the three vain attempts at conciliation Kṛṣṇa tries to make on Kaurava territory. In doing this, the avatar vindicates the right of the Pāṇḍava to get back the lands which have been unjustly seized, and declares war on the enemy. The American scholar refers also, in Dumézil fashion, to the

As for Rudra-Śiva, placed near the sacrificial stake, he represents time, which destroys and recreates without ceasing.

If Viṣṇu, the Preserver, is thus a god of space,[2] then Śiva, the Transformer, is, in contrast, a god of time. This new schema must now be related to the framework of the epic. As an avatar of Viṣṇu, Kṛṣṇa's essential mission during the war is to maintain *dharma*, or at least to preserve its efficacy until the last moments of the cycle. He cannot however avoid this deadline, which is part of a greater divine plan, and this is the reason why he never enters into direct conflict with Śiva, who, behind the scenes, is arming the warriors. This is no doubt the reason for his impartiality during the lead up to the conflict.[3] At the fateful moment when Duryodhana and Arjuna come to seek his help, the avatar immediately declares that his relationship to the Kaurava and the Pāṇḍava is identical and that he wishes them both well. These words are all the more telling, for in reality he is inarguably

---

Indo-European parentage of this myth with the rite of taking three steps into enemy territory as part of the declaration of war by the Pater Patratus, according to ancient Roman custom, as related by Livy.

2 Above all in his confrontation or complementary role to Śiva. For to the extent that he is an emanation of the Supreme Divinity, he also assumes a temporal function: 'I am the mighty world-destroying Time, now engaged in destroying the worlds, even without thee, [O Arjuna] none of the warriors arrayed in hostile armies shall live,' says Kṛṣṇa in the *Bhagavad-gītā* (11, 32).

3 Equally, his older brother Balarāma remains neutral for the whole war, and we will see in the following chapter the way he transcends the conflict.

more connected to one side than the other, for his aunt, Kuntī, is the mother of the first three Pāṇḍava and his sister is the wife of Arjuna! Significantly, Kṛṣṇa is also absent from the fateful game of dice which takes place in a typically Śivaite atmosphere: Śiva is, in fact, reputed to be a great lover of this 'past-time', so fitting in creating discord and ushering in the end of the world, while Kṛṣṇa does not hesitate on several occasions to condemn this ambiguous game. It is only when Draupadī invokes his name silently that the avatar intervenes to protect her from humiliation, in spite of the neutrality he has shown up to this point. In the same vein, we can cite the episode of the rescue *in extremis* of Parikṣit: Uttarā has to go to Kṛṣṇa to ask him to resuscitate her baby that Aśvatthāman has just killed in order to complete the revenge of the Kaurava. Now, the latter is none other than a fierce aspect of Rudra-Śiva. Describing this play of alternating influences, Hiltebeitel says:

> The *Mahābhārata* is a poem where 'all the gods' are active in human form, with Viṣṇu—incarnate in Krishna—at their head, or at their 'center', while Śiva remains typically remote until the moment when he must, after all, get his share and do his work. The relationship between Viṣṇu and Śiva is thus situated within, or 'above', the structure(s) of polytheism (1990: 356).

The contrasting roles of the two gods equally reflect the relationship that they have with the world of men, a relationship that is inscribed even in the etymology of their names. Viṣṇu, The Penetrator (very probably from the root *VIŚ*, to penetrate), acts on society from within.

As for Rudra, the Howler (from the root *RUD*, to shout, related to the Latin *rudere*, to bray, or cry like an animal, and perhaps also to *rudis*, rude, uncouth), he avoids society: he is outside it and lives in the wilderness as an ascetic.[4]

Now, the primordial forest always represents *materia prima*, the primordial chaos whose symbolism, leaving aside now the strictly academic approach, we would like to venture into more freely. It should be noted first of all that there is no shortage of literary works which start with the evocation of a forest. Such is the case of the *Divine Comedy* by Dante, with its dark forest, or the *Legend of the Grail* by Chrétien de Troyes, with his *gaste forest soutaine*, his deserted and lonely forest which refers to the forest of Brocéliande, where the knights of the Round Table gather and where Merlin and Morgan le Fay live. All these works see the light of day thanks to a creator, a poet, who transforms this chaotic matter into a cosmos and gives it order. The forest, to the extent that it is a wilderness, distinct from the place where men live, represents nature before it is transformed through art; it also represents the soul in its crude state before any initiatic rebirth.

One should add that the forest coincides with the abyss of the alchemical tradition. It is the point of departure of the Great Work, and this initiatic dimension of the creative act is always experienced inwardly by the poet, whether he is represented in his own work or not. This latter possibility, which is well known in Europe

---

4 The name Śiva is, in contrast, a euphemism. It means 'Propitious', 'Auspicious'.

because of Dante who, guided by Virgil, descends into Hell itself, not only has its parallel in India with the *Mahābhārata,* where Vyāsa plays a fundamental role, but also in the *Rāmāyaṇa*, where the gods, distressed by the sad state of the world and wishing to offer it a new path of salvation, decide to mobilise to this effect the greatest sinner in the land. They find him in the person of a terrible robber called Ratnakara, 'The Creator of a Gem', who hides in the forest waiting to kill and rob travellers. Now, when this unsavoury individual calls death to his aid by invoking '*mara, mara, mara*,' his invocation suddenly changes to *Rāma, Rāma, Rāma,* which saves him from his wickedness. He then plunges into a long meditation during which ants cover his entire body, and from which he gets his new name, Vālmīki, 'He who is covered in ants,' and in this meditation he is inspired by the gods to dictate the story of Rāma.

Pure and undifferentiated potentiality which precedes all creation is not, of course, always depicted in literature as a forest, as the last three works mentioned illustrate. Like the author of Genesis, Ovid simply describes at the beginning of *Metamorphoses* a principial formless void, without involving any metaphor. And Virgil in the *Aeneid*, as Shakespeare in *The Tempest*, speak of a storm to represent the chaos of all-possibility. In the same way, to take an example from dozens of others, one can cite the initial dream of the *Roman de la rose* of Guillaume de Lorris. But the metaphor of the forest has a particular nuance because of its symbolical and etymological ramifications. The word *matter* in fact derives from the Latin word *materia* or *materies*, itself derived from *mater*, 'mother', and it denotes originally the trunk of a tree which gives birth to offspring (cf. Spanish *madera*) and, more specifically, 'timber'. This timber then becomes the 'matter' of poets, as when one speaks of the Matter of Britain, for example, or the universal substance which philosophers contrast to form.[5] We are not able to explore here all the symbolic richness of the forest, as this would take us too far from our topic, but we will just recall that the forest setting is a common Patristic metaphor. For Origen the Scriptures are an immense wood (*latissima Scripturae silva*), for Jerome an infinite forest of meanings (*infinita sensuum silva*) which is impossible to thoroughly explore, etc; the same image, with all sorts of variations, is taken up again and again through the centuries (see Lubac, 2000: 85). Symbolism is a universal language, sometimes difficult to penetrate, but it seems impossible that the virgin forest in the *Mahābhārata* does not represent the primordial substance of a mythical treasure-trove which is both infinitely rich and inextricably complex. This fundamental notion should be kept in mind before even considering in more detail what this symbol signifies within the Indian cosmos.

If we now focus on the particular case of India, it can be argued that the forest setting (*araṇya*) is opposed to the village (*grāma*), like emptiness is to fullness. But this emptiness[6] which pulls the renouncing ascetic out

5 The Greek word *hulē*, whose rhetorical and philosophical Latin translation is the word *materia*, has as a first meaning wood as a material and wood as in forest.

6 It must be understood that this emptiness is not a nothingness: the renunciant empties himself of all worldly preoccupations in order to dedicate himself to the essential, in conformity with the Latin expression *vacare Deo*.

of the world is also that which gives, by contrast, all its meaning to the fullness of human society in the village. The *ṛṣi* of the *Mahābhārata*, unlike their predecessors, have brought their sacrificial space from the village to the forest, like the druids with their sacred glades. In this way, by immersing themselves in the sanctuary of virgin nature, they seem to be inaugurating the change in the religious perspective that will introduce the epic to the Indian world. The story framework of the *Mahābhārata* takes on yet another dimension if we consider what Michel Angot says about the polarity between emptiness and fullness in Indian society:

> For the forest is the other world, the place of the absolute: *para* 'other' [...] means also the transcendent. This is the reason why it is in the forest that those who renounce the world must stay in order to fully seek solitude and abandon the *dharma* of the laws of society. Over time the polarity between these two spaces has never ceased, but it has changed: in the *Veda*, the world of the village is that of the sacrifice and is thus positive, the forest being negative. In Hinduism the importance of renunciation and *yoga* has reversed these poles (2001: 100–101).

This reversal in values also signifies something else that one should not lose sight of. In the time of the *dvāpara-yuga*, the Bronze Age, normal integration into the community did not pose the same dangers of worldly delusion as exist now in the *kali-yuga*. It is due to the corruption of time that, in the last age, the hermit's life is in principle safer than life among men. However, and this is one of the main functions of the *Mahābhārata* and, spiritually speaking, *a fortiori*, the *Bhagavad-gītā*, the fact remains as Biardeau says, 'One has to reconcile the perennial nature of the world—no one wants to see it end!—with finding the possibility of a definitive personal salvation' (1985: 1, 29). That the forest setting becomes, *par excellence*, the place for initiatic trials and the maturation that they imply is even more telling in the epic in that it is precisely in the heart of this solitude, in a context of total destitution, that the Pāṇḍava are forced to live out their exile and where they receive many important lessons from different sages.

We have seen that the Indologists, while failing to insist on the symbolic nature of the primordial forest, have, however, perfectly understood that the epic, recited during a Vedic *sattra*, is grafted somehow on to it and is nourished by its sap. They have also shown that in renewing the form of the sacrifice and situating it in the forest, the epic confers on this rite a new meaning. One can also say that the *Mahābhārata* is itself substituted for the Vedic sacrifice. And the purificatory and initiatic value that becomes its own and which it appears to provide in an act of self-justification is the subject of much comment at the end of the book. Thus the penultimate *śloka* says, 'He who hears and recites this text assiduously to others is freed from all his sins and obtains the state (*pada*) of Viṣṇu.'

Finally the forest which sees, so to speak, the flowering of the *Mahābhārata* has a very interesting name. It is called Naimiṣa, the forest of the 'blink of an eye' (*nimeṣa*), for it is said that an army of *asura*, demons, was once destroyed there in the blink of an eye. The association with the battle of Kurukṣetra is obvious, but this blink of an eye which opens onto a world reborn refers also to the timelessness of the beginning of creation which springs from nothing, *ex nihilo*, like the spark coming from nowhere at the tip of the flint.[7] It is interesting to note that *nimeṣa* is also the smallest measurement of time in traditional India. A day consisting of 24 hours (= 86,400 seconds) is made up of 30 *muhūrta* consisting of 2,880 seconds; a *muhūrta* is made up of 30 *kalā* consisting of 96 seconds; a *kalā* of 30 *kāṣṭā* of 3.2 seconds; and a *kāṣṭā* of 18 *nimeṣa* of 0.1777... second (cf. *Mānavadharmaśāstra*, 1, 64). What better place than the forest of a blink of an eye could thus serve as the background for this original *fiat lux*, this fabulous revelation, which is the birth of the epic into the spiritual cosmos of India? We will have ample opportunity to see later that with the theory of the four ages and its indefinite extensions, the *Mahābhārata* situates itself in time in a unique way, and this is one of the most important contributions of this text to the earlier Vedic tradition.

7 D.G. White sees in this blink, very poetically, an allusion to the shimmering of the stars in the winter night which covers the forest in question. The stars, particularly the Milky Way, represent the souls of the fallen in the battle of Kurukṣetra, heroically killed in combat (cited by Hiltebeitel 2001:158).

7

The Concept of the Avatar

FROM THE POINT of view of the history of religions, the major event which accompanied the birth of Indian mythology in the *Mahābhārata* was the emergence of the idea of the avatar, unknown to the Vedic world. An *avatāra* is literally a descent (of a god to earth), and even though the epic does not use this term yet (it only uses the verb *ava-TṚ*, to descend), Viṣṇu appears explicitly as such in the person of Kṛṣṇa. One can see in this concept of descent a logical consequence of the principle mentioned above (ch. 5), according to which the Vedic gods served as models for the heroes. But this tells us nothing about the religious, philosophical and metaphysical dimensions which this new idea covers. Biardeau remains very embarrassed when she tries to explain this issue:

> Certainly we can credit the genius who imagined the war of the Bhārata and the events surrounding it to having a powerful synthesising intelligence. However, the invention *ex nihilo* of the *avatāra*, the 'descent' of the supreme divinity to earth

> and his essential relationship with the ideal king cannot be ascribed to him. Now the *avatāra* of Viṣṇu, Kṛṣṇa, appears explicitly as such for the first time in the epic, as well as his human-divine link to Arjuna who incarnates the perfect prince. We can only conjecture an historical link between the *upaniṣad* debates of the Brahmins and *kṣatriya* and this descent of Viṣṇu into the world of men in a new divine form. In fact more or less direct references can be found to the *upaniṣad* in the *MBh*.... But these intertextual references, important and decisive as they may be in understanding the intentions of the poet of the epic, say nothing whatsoever about the *avatāra* (1985: 1, 28–29).

In fact we are forced to turn to the field of comparative religion to understand and comment on this 'invention *ex nihilo* of the *avatāra*, the "descent" of the supreme divinity to earth' which the French scholar cannot attribute to the 'genius who imagined the war of the Bhārata.' Let us look at what transpired in Greece. The heroes of the *Iliad* are often depicted as 'demi-gods' like the protagonists of the Indian epic. Thus Achilles belongs to the race of Zeus by his father and is the son of the sea nymph Thetis, herself the daughter of Oceanus, the god of the Ocean. Hector is, according to certain ancient traditions, the son of Apollo, and Aeneas is the son of Venus, etc. This type of divine affiliation extends, in the Graeco-Roman civilisation, even to historical figures, if legends like the one recounted by Diogenes Laertius about Plato are taken into account:

> When Perictione was old enough for marriage, Ariston wanted to make violent love to her, but he did not succeed; once his violence ceased, he had a vision of the face of Apollo, who by means of this apparition preserved Perictione's virginity until her child was born... Plato was born on the 88th Olympiad, on 7th May, the anniversary of the same day that Apollo himself was born at Delphi.[1]

Pythagoras, for his part, was the son of Hermes (*ibid.*, II, 126), and nearly five centuries later, Apollonius of Tyana (d. 97 AD) was still considered by some to be the son of Zeus Keeper-of-Oaths (Philostratus 6). As for Caesar, he is reputed to be, as a descendant of Aeneas, a son of Venus.[2] But neither in Greece nor in Rome, *a fortiori*, did they go so far as to include in their theology the concept of a full incarnation of the supreme deity, and this is perhaps the reason why these two traditions could not sustain the relationship between myth and religion, as we noticed at the end of chapter 4. If the concept of the divine unity was no stranger to them, as evidenced by the majority of philosophical currents which flourished at that time, the political, rather than the soteriological nature of their respective religions, seems to have pre-

---

1 *Lives of Eminent Philosophers*, I, ed. R.D. Hicks.

2 Nearly all the great saints of Hindu India are considered to be at least partial avatars of certain divinities of the pantheon right up to the present day. For example, Rāmakṛṣṇa (19th century) is taken to be a manifestation of Kālī, and Ramaṇa Maharṣi (20th century) of Murugan, as Skanda or Kārttikeya is called in Tamil areas. It should be noted that it is not rare, as in the first example, for a goddess to incarnate as a male or the reverse.

vented this possibility,[3] and perhaps was the main cause of their decline in the face of the widespread dissemination of Christianity. For it is to this new belief, within a non Indo-European tradition, that one must turn to find, and in a historical way too, an equivalent of the avataric function of Kṛṣṇa. Such indeed is Christ, whose role within the Trinity is to be the incarnation of the divine Plenitude. The fact that the appearance of these two major figures of religious consciousness, Jesus and Kṛṣṇa, was nearly contemporaneous can only be interpreted from the traditional point of view as a 'sign of the times'. The numerous analogies which can be found between them have certainly caused much ink to flow. And even if certain points of comparison, like a pseudo-etymology common to the names of Christos and Kṛṣṇa, refers to a weak and debatable hermeneutics, it nevertheless remains the case that they share a number of traits in common: they were both born miraculously at midnight of royal descent, they were both persecuted in their childhood, both were the cause of a massacre of innocents which forced them into hiding, they were taken in by shepherds, and so on. More fundamentally, their teachings preach a complete devotion to the incarnate divinity, a way of love, and both offer as a principal means of spiritual realisation the continuous invocation of their Names. This was enough for certain early Orientalists to

[3] It is interesting that while Zeus (or Jupiter) is not the originator of a theophanic manifestation of the supreme divinity, despite his preeminent position in the pantheon, neither is his Vedic equivalent, Indra; for it is Viṣṇu who plays this role in Hinduism, even though he appears in the *Veda* as a lieutenant to the king of the gods.

imagine that the *Mahābhārata* had an influence on early Christianity,[4] and this notwithstanding the most significant differences between the two theophanies, such as the Hindu avatar's multitude of marriages and the total absence of any form of the Passion in his life.

It is true that Christians have, in the course of their history, universally denied in principle the validity of other religions and that the vast majority of them find it impossible to admit that God could incarnate, in the fullest sense of the word, in a person other than Christ. The mythological character of the life of Kṛṣṇa, where the marvelous is expressed on a scale of immediate improbability far beyond the miracles of Jesus, and the absence of a doctrine based on the Resurrection, obviously does not help matters. The 'historical' argument remains for them decisive, to the extent that they cannot conceive at all that the Word could be made flesh in a person without a historical substance, whatever the truth and beauty of the teachings which result from this might be. The inverse, however, is quite different. Hindus never hesitate to describe Christ as an avatar due to their inclusive attitude vis-à-vis the Christian way. This is evident for example in this quotation by Rāmakṛṣṇa: 'The Avatar is always the same. The One God plunges into the ocean of life, incarnates and his name is Krishna. At another time he plunges, comes up in another place amongst humanity and his name is Jesus' (Herbert [1949] 1972: 340). And

---

[4] For example Bentley, cited by Wiseman in his *Discours sur les rapports entre la science et la religion révélée*, which contains some useful and curious information on the trials and errors of Orientalists confronted with the Indian tradition for the first time (1845: 267).

this teaching of the Bengali saint finds a perfect echo in the words of the metaphysician Guénon:

> I must also draw your attention to the fact that the religious point of view is necessarily linked to certain historical contingencies, while the metaphysical point of view refers exclusively to the principial order. If you speak of 'multiple avatars', it means you are speaking from the standpoint of the world of appearance; but in absolute reality, they are 'the same'; the Christ-principle is not multiple, whatever be its terrestrial or other manifestations. The 'Mediator', according to all traditions, is the 'Universal Man' who is also Christ; and whatever name he may be called changes nothing, and I do not see what difficulty there is in that.[5]

Before proceeding further in these reflections on the metaphysical implications contained in the idea of the avatar and examining the scope that traditional exegesis has played concerning this phenomenon, we would like to develop some further considerations on the horizontal or, rather, historical causality which precipitated the emergence of this new spiritual possibility. All traditions teach that a new Revelation, whatever it may be, comes from 'on high', and that because of this it transcends history. It is no less true that, on the one hand, a divine intervention is necessarily linked to the specific conditions of a given time, and that, on the other hand, this

---

[5] Translated from a letter dated 23 February, 1934, to R. Martínez Espinosa: Guénon, 2013: 238.

intervention has to be situated at a point along a historical continuum which forces it to take account of the preceding events associated with the milieu in which it arises. To say that avatars are born into a family and therefore have a family tree is incidentally proof of this. This inclusion within a specific world is the very principle of religious 'forms' intended to be more or less universally received according to the inevitable limitations associated with these same forms, which are a necessary response to the diversity of human types. These limitations are also largely based on the language and culture which conveys the Revelation. Because we are dealing mainly with Hinduism here, it must be remembered that this tradition presupposes a particular environment and, above all, the durability of its caste system which inevitably restricted its dissemination, notwithstanding the multitude of doctrinal and cultural variations it contains. What Christianity had to do in relation to Judaism and the ancient religions, and what Islam had to do with regard to Christianity and Judaism (not to mention Sabaism), Hinduism also had to do, according to the same logic, with regard to the Vedic religion and Buddhism.

If we return now to Biardeau's argument which sees in the *Mahābhārata*, and consequently in Hindu *bhakti*, a brahmanic reaction to the widespread expansion of Buddhism in India, it can be concluded, following her historicising point of view and although she does not go this far, that the idea of the avatar was 'suggested' to Brahmanism (unless it imposed itself as such) because of the importance that the Buddha[6] had assumed in his-

[6] Certain scholars who have been keen to deny the historical reality of the Buddha have had, it is true, a bit more credibility

tory. Although born in the Indian spiritual cosmos, the Awakened One eminently synthesised in his person an original position differing totally from the Vedic tradition, and it is no exaggeration to say that the appearance of a spiritual master of such magnitude demanded an adequate response on the same plane: Kṛṣṇa, born to a *kṣatriya* milieu like the Buddha, somehow neutralised the character of the latter's teachings, deemed heretical, by bringing everything back to a brahmanic orthodoxy and saving the principle of caste, which had been threatened by an inclusive doctrine rooted in monasticism. We know that the Buddha would later be included on the list of the ten most important avatars of Viṣṇu, which was a simple way for the Hindu tradition to 'relativise' Buddhism—being unable to ignore it completely—spiritually and historically speaking.[7] The simple fact that in the mythic

---

than those who have denied the historical reality of Jesus. But even if it is admitted that their legends and hagiography have changed the perception we have of these masters of wisdom, the traditional perspective remains nonetheless what it is. That Kṛṣṇa Devakīputra (the son of Devakī) is also mentioned in the *Chāndogyopaniṣad* (3, 17, 6), a text disseminated at an earlier time, in principle, than the life of the Buddha, does not at all invalidate what can be said about the role that Kṛṣṇa was called upon to play after the composition of the epic.

[7] Buddhism continues to annoy the pietistic *bhakti* of modern India. It is not without interest to see how certain writers resolve the problem, strange as their arguments may seem: 'In the same *Śrīmad-Bhāgavatam* where Lord Buddha is accepted as an incarnation of Kṛṣṇa it is stated that Lord Buddha appeared in order to bewilder the atheistic class of men. Therefore his philosophy is meant for bewildering the atheists and should not be accepted. If someone asks why should Kṛṣṇa propagate atheistic principles the answer is that it was the desire of the

chronology of the *Purāṇa*, Kṛṣṇa is listed as an avatar before the Buddha, as a reminder of a reality englobing the Buddhist perspective, seems to corroborate this hypothesis. In addition, it should be noted that Buddhism did not stay inactive faced with this Hindu offensive. The appearance of an iconography of the Buddha, still unknown at the time of Sāñcī (third century BC), dates from the beginning of the Christian era, and introduced into this tradition a form of image worship which answered in its own way to the rival development of such worship in Hinduism. That this iconography betrays in the art of Gandhara an indisputable influence of Greek statuary is also a very remarkable thing.

A similar phenomenon, in the reaction of an ancient tradition facing the eruption of a new religion of growing importance, is also evident in the unusual figure of Apollonius of Tyana, already mentioned above. Christian apologists since Eusebius of Caesarea (end of the third, beginning of the fourth century AD) denounced this sage as a counterfeit Christ who had been invented by the Greeks to rival Jesus. Although Pierre Grimal (1958: 1028) may well deny any false intention of this nature on the part of Philostratus, who related the life of this Pythagorean sage, it nevertheless remains that

---

Supreme Personality of the Godhead to end the violence which was then being committed in the name of the Vedas. The so-called religionists were falsely using the Vedas to justify such violent acts as meat eating, and Lord Buddha came to lead the people away from such a false interpretation of the Vedas. Also for the atheists Lord Buddha preached atheism so that they would follow him and thus be tricked into devotional service to Lord Buddha or Kṛṣṇa' (Swami Prabhupāda, 1985: 61).

the Christians, on the one hand, really did see what they had seen and that, on the other hand, no other Greek miracle-worker performed so many miracles that so closely paralleled those of Jesus. If the idea of 'counterfeiting' has something useless and despicable about it and reflects the vanity of interconfessional strife, it remains that Apollonius was like the swan-song of the spiritual tradition of the ancient Greeks, and his spiritual personality was really an echo of the emerging Christian religion. As for the Brahmins that Apollonius visited, they seem, as was their habit, to have easily discerned an avataric quality in him. Once again it all seems to be 'in tune with the times'.

Turning now to the principal metaphysical implications of the concept of the avatar, we can start from the idea that this possibility stems from the fact that God has created man in his own image and that He is therefore inclined, logically speaking, to take on the form of his creature to remind him of this truth whenever it becomes necessary. In the *Bhagavad-gītā*, Kṛṣṇa declares to Arjuna: 'O descendent of Bharata, whenever there is a decline in *dharma*, and an ascendancy in *adharma*, then I manifest Myself' (4, 7). Hence one can see the causal relationship which necessarily exists between a fall inexorably involving humanity and a divine descent among men. Certainly, Viṣṇu does not always manifest himself in human form, since sometimes he appears as an animal or semi-animal, but one must be aware of the symbolism in such cases, and it is possible that there is, in the gradual humanising of the avataric function, a sign of the loss of a consciousness of the transparency of phenomena over the course of time. 'The tortoise, for example, in its ability to interiorise and exteriorise at will, symbolises primordial man at the threshold of inner and outer manifestation/non-manifestation, who in the role of vicegerent, as we have seen, is invested with the responsibility for upholding cosmic order' (Perry, 1995: 54). The Lakota Indians of North America, Sitting Bull, Black Elk and Crazy Horse, significantly remained faithful to this symbolic intimacy with the animal kingdom. What, above all, makes man in the image of God is the deiform faculty of the intellect, both 'uncreated and uncreatable' according to Meister Eckhart, which permits him to participate in the divine Subject. Now, the *avatāra* plays an analogous role in the Creation to that of the intellect in man. Revelation, which is synthesised in the person of the avatar, reinstates man in his capacity as viceregent of Creation and offers him a way to remember this intrinsic function and assume it fully. As Frithjof Schuon says:

> By the 'fall', Intellect, which in itself is universal, is 'individualised' and replaced by the reason, while Creation, which at the outset was conceived by man as 'interior', has been 'exteriorised' and has become the material world. The *Avatara*, in 'subjectifying' the Universe and in 'objectifying' the Intellect, restores to man in a certain way his primordial quality of effective and conscious manifestation of the divine. Creation is what is most 'exterior'; the two poles meet completely in the *Avatara*, who thus unites in his person both the totality of the 'objective' macrocosm, and the centre of the 'subjective' microcosm (1961: 89).

It is in this sense, what is more, that Christ, as a divine incarnation, could be compared to the cornerstone once rejected but now returned to the head of the corner. It should also be noted that if according to traditional thought, in India as elsewhere, the descent of the soul of an ordinary individual enters into a previously formed embryo (which explains the diverse attitudes of tolerance towards an abortion carried out before this descent occurs), the avatar descends into the world from the time of his conception, whether he is immediately born at that time, like Vyāsa, or whether he follows the normal way of a gestation *in utero*. The dogma of the Annunciation (thc actual conception of Jesus) and of the Immaculate Conception (the conception of Mary) specifically illustrate this point in the Christian context.

In the last part of the preceding paragraph we have mostly been following the teachings of Schuon, who has synthesised in a few illuminating pages (*ibid.* 112 and following) the doctrine of the avatar beyond its simple and unique application to the Hindu tradition. The same author then develops a typology of avatars whom he divides into major and plenary (mainly the founders of religions whose influence radiates over sometimes thousands of years) and minor and partial (the secondary prophets, saints and sages who transmit in some way the function of the first kind and revive the tradition in which they live), these two groups being, for him, subdivided into solar and lunar types. We refer the reader desiring to know more on this subject to his works, and meanwhile we will return to the case of the *Mahābhārata* which is our main focus here. Above (ch. 3) we looked at the close relationship between Kṛṣṇa and Arjuna, and we will discuss this further in the following chapter. For now we will examine the link between Kṛṣṇa and his older brother Balarāma. When Vasudeva and Devakī, Kṛṣṇa's parents, are imprisoned by the imposter Kaṃsa, this villainous king, warned by a voice from heaven that an offspring of his cousin will bring about his destruction, systematically murders her newborn babies one after the other until finally this unhappy woman is able to miraculously and secretly transfer her seventh embryo into the womb of Rohinī, her co-wife, who has come to visit her in prison. Thus is born Balarāma, the brother, or half-brother, of Kṛṣṇa. As for Kṛṣṇa, he escapes from Kamsa's vengeance later in an almost equally wonderful way, when a supernatural stupor overcomes the guards, enabling Vasudeva to leave the palace prison temporarily so that he can go and take his newborn son to the cow herder Nanda.[8] Now, Balarāma is also considered to be an *avatāra* of Viṣṇu, and the *Viṣṇu-purāṇa* (5, 1, 59–63) tells us that he was born from a white hair pulled from the god's head, whereas Kṛṣṇa was born from a black hair. The two brothers therefore share the same avataric function, and in the Puranic list of the ten major avatars they appear together in eighth place, at least if they are not separate, in which case Kṛṣṇa is moved to ninth at the expense of the Buddha, who then disappears from the list altogether. Balarāma in this way embodies the serpent Śeṣa or Ananta, on whom Viṣṇu Nārāyaṇa rests during the cosmic night between two creations of the world. Śeṣa means the Rest and Ananta the Infinite.

---

[8] On this episode in the *Harivaṃśa*, and especially its parallel with the story of the Holy Innocents, cf. *The Queen and the Avatar*, p. 36.

Balarāma thus represents the infinite 'substance' of the divinity through or in which the creative and 'essential' power of the Absolute manifests itself. He also incarnates the Remains of past worlds, witness of the co-eternity of manifestation in relation to the principle. We have discovered, in *The Queen and the Avatar*, a parallel between Balarāma and John the Baptist, the cousin of Jesus, who ensures within the Christian framework a link between the Old Law and the New. The camaraderie between Balarāma and Kṛṣṇa, having fun together as children in the vicinity of the Vṛndāvana forest, thus likewise readily evokes the image of John the Baptist and Jesus playing together at the same age.

We have not yet discussed, except in passing, a teaching of the utmost importance, which is that, by his birth, the avatar offers man the sacrament of his Name which mysteriously contains all that he is, and consequently, the essence of divinity itself. This aspect of things is most of the time passed over in silence in the scientific literature of Indologists. This fundamental doctrine is, however, essential, and leads to *japa-yoga*, the continuous invocation of the divine Name. The attitude of the Hindu invoking Kṛṣṇa or Rāma is, without doubt, the same as that of believers of all creeds who accept the identity between God and his Name as the basis of a practice of jaculatory prayer. Here is Schuon again:

> There is a prayer where God Himself is in a sense the Subject, and that is the pronouncing of a revealed divine Name. The foundation of this mystery is, on the one hand, that 'God and his Name are one' (Ramakrishna), and on the

> other, that God Himself pronounces His Name in Himself, hence in eternity and outside of all creation, so that His unique and uncreated word is the prototype of jaculatory prayer and even, in a less direct sense, of all prayer (1961: 128).

In another work, the same author stresses the invocation of the divine Name in Christianity, Buddhism and Hinduism. Regarding the latter he quotes the *Viṣṇudharmottara*, a Kasmiri treatise from about the sixth century which says,

> That which is obtained by meditation in the age of *Krita*, by sacrifice in the age of *Treta*, by devotion in the age of *Dwapara*, is obtained in the *Kali* age by celebrating *Keshava* (Vishnu)... The repetition of His Name, O *Maitreya*, is for faults the equivalent of fire for metals... Water suffices to put out fire, the sunrise to disperse the darkness; in the *Kali* age, the repetition of the Name of *Hari* (*Vishnu*) suffices to destroy all errors (1953: 191).[9]

This is in fact a common saying in Puranic literature—which perhaps Schuon did not know when he chose this quotation—since the same verse appears, with small variations, in several texts more or less contemporary

9 The author shows that this doctrine of the invocation as a primary way of salvation can be found also in the traditions which do not have an avatar, such as Islam, which uses divine names for this purpose. Incidentally, the word god (like the German *Gott*) is the past participle of a root meaning 'to call, invoke'. God is thus defined here as the Invoked.

to the *Viṣṇudharmottara*.[10] In any case, this teaching eloquently emphasises the close connection between the coming of an avatar, the *kali-yuga* and invocation as a means of salvation.

One important consequence of this doctrine of the invocation is that the Hindu tradition has kept as a particularly efficacious practice the simultaneous invocation of Names referring to a double theophany such as those relating to the above mentioned Rāma (Balarāma) and Kṛṣṇa. The invocation of Rāma-Kṛṣṇa or, as in a more widespread and longer formula: *Hare Kṛṣṇa Hare Kṛṣṇa Kṛṣṇa Kṛṣṇa Hare Hare, Hare Rāma Hare Rāma Rāma Rāma Hare Hare*,[11] is thus highly recommended. That the avatar manifested under a dual aspect demands a double invocation should not be surprising, for certain Vedic hymns were already addressed to Mitra-Varuṇa, as we have seen above, and Christianity has the same practice with the association of the names of Jesus and Mary (*Iesu-Maria*).[12] The Hindu tradition has other examples of such combinations, notably in the 'marital' invoca-

---

10 Particularly in the *Viṣṇu-purāṇa*, 6, 2, 17 (5th) and the *Bhāgavata-purāṇa*, 12, 3, 52 (10th): cf. González-Reimann, 2010: 174.

11 This invocation is taken from the *Brahmāṇḍa-purāṇa* and was popularised by the Bengali saint Caitanya (15–16th centuries). It also contains another name of Kṛṣṇa, Hari (Hare in the vocative). Rāma designates here the Balarāma of the *Mahābhārata*, and not Rāmacandra the hero of the *Rāmāyaṇa*, as is sometimes thought.

12 On another slightly different note, the prophetic function is sometimes shared, as in the Bible where Moses and Aaron share the same mission in complementary fashion.

tions of Lakṣmī-Nārāyaṇa, Sītā-Rāma, Rādhā-Kṛṣṇa and Rādhā-Mādhava (another name for Kṛṣṇa), Sītā and Rādhā being *avatāra* of the goddess Lakṣmī, the consort of Viṣṇu-Nārāyaṇa. In the case where, as here, a god is associated with his wife as his *śakti*, her name in the Indian tradition will always precede the name of the god. Mention should also be made in this context of the invocation Hari-Hara, which plays on a paronomasia, uniting the names of Kṛṣṇa and Śiva.

8

The *Bhagavad-gītā* and the Sacrificial War

THE *BHAGAVAD-GĪTĀ* corresponds to chapters 24 to 42 of the *Bhīṣmaparvan*, book 6 of the *Mahābhārata*. It recounts, in a scene often represented in works of art, the dialogue between Kṛṣṇa and Arjuna which takes place on the chariot they share, on the eve of the decisive battle of Kurukṣetra. The two armies are face to face, ready to do battle, but on seeing the enemy army he is about to fight, full of his uncles, cousins and even his own guru, the master of arms, Droṇa, Arjuna falls prey to a terrible depression. The immediate justification behind the words of the avatar in this tragic context stems from the need for the Pāṇḍava clan to overcome the hesitation of their best warrior. But the philosophical, religious or mystical content of Kṛṣṇa's discourse takes on a universal dimension as the avatar seals his teaching with a sort of Transfiguration: for he reveals himself to his companion in his multiple cosmic form, which at the same time overwhelms Arjuna and puts an end once and for all to any reluctance he has left to accomplish his duty.

Something important distinguishes the traditional approach from the scientific analysis of texts, as dissected by most philologists, historians of religion and modern commentators. Whereas the generality of believers instinctively perceive a global coherence in sacred writings, punctilious researchers only see disparate sources and many contradictions due to the influences of various concurrent schools of thought.[1] Thus the *Mahābhārata*, in general, and the *Bhagavad-gītā*, in particular, have been subjected to the same treatment as the Bible and the Gospels in the West, which have been shaken to their very foundations by a severe criticism only too anxious to find in their composition the basic incoherence of a fabrication. If not simply discarded as clumsy, this supposed fabrication calls at least for structural rereadings which

[1] For example, Sénart: 'The doctrine of the Bhagavad-gītā is not presented in a methodical, organically organised way. It unfolds very loosely. Assuredly, at times there is a concern to connect the dialogue with the givens of a scene in which it is quite artificially embedded; but on the whole ideas come and go without an exact sequence; repetitions abound and some developments are given full reign out of all proportion to the doctrinal importance of the subjects they touch on and statements clash and contradict each other. It is hard to believe that such obvious disparities are the work of one author. It has been supposed that the poem as we know it is the result of a reworking: a primitive text was subsequently rewritten at the hands of a rival philosophy which made changes and essential additions' (1967:VI), and so on. The two rival schools imagined by this author are the monist *Vedānta* and the dualist *Sāṃkhya*. That said, the disparity of the four Gospels and the absence of a systematic discourse in the Qur'an have not led astray Christians and Muslims any more than the 'clutter' perceived by Sénart in the *Bhagavad-gītā* has led Hindus astray.

inevitably cast doubt on the harmonious unity seen in these texts by the *homo religiosus*. Even if in the traditional world it is admitted that a sacred book like the Bible or the *Veda* could have been successively 'elaborated on' by a number of authors, the faith in a Revelation, considered as monolithic by the believers, is conceived by most scholars in an anthropological and sociological light. They like to point out the endless groping of a credulous humanity in its desperate and vain desire to find a meaning to life through the supernatural. In cases like these, it is not uncommon for them to judge that the texts in question have been subjected to some form of manipulation completely devoid of spiritual motives.

These two opposing tendencies have led to the debates we have alluded to regarding the sole or multiple authorship of the *Mahābhārata*, and we have seen that the research of Orientalists has tended gradually, over the years, to adopt a more conciliatory position vis à vis the strongly held convictions of the Indian tradition. The same is true with regard to the particular status of the *Bhagavad-gītā*, which lies at the heart of the epic, together with the concomitant question of its dating. The literature on this subject is enormous, and one can find in it pretty much anything one wants. If, in fact, one considers *The Song of the Lord*, for that is the meaning of the title of this part of the epic, as an addition to the story about the war of the Bhārata, one can equally well see it as being the insertion of a preexisting text, or, as happens quite frequently, as the incorporation of a later gloss, in which some have even gone so far as to detect a Christian influence! Some Indian scholars have in fact adopted the first hypothesis and have put the composition of the *Gītā* at a very early date, such as, for instance, B. G. Tilak, who places it at 3,100 BC, whereas others who are more modest, like S. Radhakrishnan, have put it in the fifth century BC, at about the time of the composition of the majority of the *Upaniṣad* and the life of the Buddha.[2] In doing so, they rely on the fact that in the text—for them at least, because the point is disputed—there is no explicit reference to the latter's teachings.

The mention here of the *Upaniṣad* takes on a particular significance, to the extent that, traditionally, the dialogue between Kṛṣṇa and Arjuna is formally attached to this sacred corpus. Witness the colophons of most of the manuscripts which have passed down with it and which refer to it as 'The Treatise on *Yoga* of the sacred *Upaniṣad* of the Song of the Lord, of the knowledge of *brahman* (*brahma-vidyā*).' This means that this part of the epic is considered by Hindus as belonging to *śruti* and not *smṛti*, as we saw above (ch. 2), and that they believe it to be the result of direct revelation, which, one must remember, does not prevent them from discerning in it doctrinal, ritual and other 'sources' which root it within its specific tradition.[3] But the *Bhagavad-gītā* does,

---

2 We have based ourselves here on the introduction by Jean M. Rivière to his excellent French translation of the *Gītā* (1979). What he says in this part of his book is no doubt far from being an actual and adequate description of contemporary research, but it is not our intention to go into that debate in detail.

3 This way of seeing things always provokes defensive reflexes in pietist circles. But there is no sacred text which is not expressed in a particular language, with all its limitations and varied hues, linked to the culture which gives rise to it. Revelation grafts itself onto the earthly condition of the people it addresses.

none the less, present a hitherto unusual way of seeing things, and the religion of *bhakti* that it generates is essentially new. And as Madeleine Biardeau concludes in her academic research on the sources, 'In connection with these new cultural practices, we will never know where the completed doctrine presented in the *Bhagavad-gītā*, which lies at the heart of the story [of the *Mahābhārata*], springs from' (1985: 1, 29). In contrast, she ultimately accepts the traditional point of view when she affirms, very fortunately, that, 'As for depriving the "original" MBh of the diamond of the Bhagavad-gītā, as has been dared so many times up to the present, it would be absurd; it would be like raising a building before laying its foundations' (*ibid.*, 28).

We do not wish to expound too much here on the teachings of the *Bhagavad-gītā*. It is easy to find abundant literature on it, but we will simply touch on some factors which for Hindus furnish crucial keys to the epic. The first thing to mention is that the text is addressed to a *kṣatriya*, that is to a man who is anything but a monk, and whose status as a warrior obliges him to act. He is subject to the law of *karman*, the law of action, and his salvation, his deliverance (*mokṣa*), necessarily requires an accurate understanding of his function in the world, his *svadharma*, his personal *dharma*. Now, the context in which a warrior acts is, by definition, the battlefield, and the war of Kurukṣetra is by no means a trivial conflict. For the Hindu it obviously symbolises the human condition. There is here a Heraclitean intuition that sees the world as an incessant struggle between opposing forces from which man cannot escape, since the fight itself is 'the Father of all things.'[4] The battlefield, from this perspective, takes on an initiatic dimension, and Kṛṣṇa teaches Arjuna nothing other than a way of realisation of the self, or rather the Self, whose touchstone is renunciation, not of the acts themselves, but of their fruits. This is what is called *niṣkāma-karman*, or *phala-tṛṣṇa-vairāgya*, the act accomplished without any egotistical desire for its fruits. Thus the avatar instructs his friend, who will become his most faithful devotee, his *bhakta*, 'always be focused on action alone, never on the fruit of action. Do not let the goal of your acts be their fruits, neither give way to inaction' (*Bhagavad-gītā*, 2, 47). This is the real meaning of the sacrificial dimension of the war, revised and corrected in the perspective of *bhakti*. Biardeau says,

> One is here at the kernel of the MBh's plot. Its great problem is about action—*karman* <*kṛ-*, 'to do'—whose model is the ritual act. If one is able to detach the ritual act, necessary in the world, from the desire for personal results, the rite ceases to stick to its agent and its future consequences will be of no concern to him and will not bind him to the world of rebirth. Otherwise said, it is possible to continue to perform ritual activity in conformity with our state, while seeking our final deliverance (1985: 1, 35).

That the epic transposes the Vedic sacrifice onto another plane through its narrative form is a point upon which both tradition and scholarly criticism now firmly

[4] Cf., among others, fragments 8, 53 and 80 from the edition by Diels-Kranz.

agree. Regarding this, Angelika Malinar (2012: 57) raises a very important point:

> Even Duryodhana, in the opposite camp to the Pāṇḍava, sees in the battle nothing other than a *raṇa-yajña*, a war sacrifice: 'The chariot is the altar, the sword the sacrificial spoon, the club the ladle, the armour the sacrificial assembly, the four horses are the four priests, the arrows the *darbha*[5] grass, fame the oblation. Having offered up ourselves to Manu Vaivasvata in this battle, O king [Dhṛtarāṣṭra], we will win and return, covered with glory, the enemies slain.'

As for Danielle Feller, she summarises the whole question quoting this same passage, then another longer one on the same topic, where Karṇa expresses a similar view. Then she adds: 'It is rather curious that these sacrificial descriptions of the war to come are placed in the mouths of those who will lose the war' (2004: 257). What seems on the narrative plane to be ironic, demonstrates, no doubt, that the nature of this war is 'objectively' sacrificial; that is, that it appears as such even to those who do not know that it is they who will be its victims and not the sacrificants. And, as Coomaraswamy says, 'In reality, Slayer and Dragon, sacrificer and victim are *One* in spirit behind the scenes, where there is no polarity of contraries, but mortal enemies on the stage, where the everlasting war of the Gods and the Titans is displayed' (1971: 7).

---

5 *Dharba* or *kuśa* is a sacred plant used in certain Brahmanic rites and is reminiscent, because of its rigidity and pointed end, of an arrow.

The fact that in the story of the epic the sacrificial act is envisaged, *a priori*, from the point of view of a *kṣatriya*, justifies, in its way, the use of violence, so abhorred by Buddhists. But this violence is not gratuitous; it is part of a necessity of the type *si vis pacem para bellum* at the service of upholding *dharma*, or at least what is left of it in the troubled times that the epic reflects. This is why Bhīṣma, the ancestor (*pitāmaha*, literally grandfather) of all the fighters, who has renounced marriage and power and who is obliged to fight on the 'bad' side with the Kaurava because of his unwavering allegiance to them, recalls this truth at the point of his death on his bed of arrows.[6] He addresses Yudhiṣṭhira who, though belonging to the opposing side, waits on him during this trial with the utmost veneration and devotion:

> I do not see anyone surviving in this world by observing *ahiṃsa* [non-violence]. In reality, the strongest live off the weak. The mongoose eats the mouse and the cat eats the mongoose. The dog eats the cat as the beast eats the dog, and man devours them all. See how time passes, and how all creatures whether mobile or not serve as food for life. He who knows that things

---

[6] Let us recall that Bhīṣma has received, thanks to his double renunciation, the power to choose the moment of his death. He has been defeated by the Pāṇḍava who have riddled him with arrows to the point where he lies suspended above the ground as if on a bed. The arrows keep him from touching the Earth which drinks the blood of the fighters and on which he must die. Bhīṣma stoically waits for the end of the battle and then gives his last teaching to his nephew, whom he still cherishes, even though he fought against him in the war.

> have been thus arranged by *daiva* ['Destiny', that which comes from the gods and the dice] is not misled. Be what you were created to be, O Prince. For fools, with their anger and joy controlled, who flee to the forest like ascetics, can only live by killing... (cited and translated originally by Biardeau, 2002: 1, 156).

To the non-acting Buddhist is thus opposed a morality that does not dispense with violence when it is required for the sake of upholding *dharma*.

Now, *dharma* is not something immutable in time. It is also subject to periodic redefinition according to the progressive degeneration of the conditions pertaining to humanity, and to the situation in which we find ourselves from one moment to the next. Hiltebeitel says, 'The highest dharma seems to be knowing the highest dharma for whatever particular situation one is in, and recognizing that situation within an ontology that admits virtually endless variation...' (2001: 208). It is therefore particularly interesting to see how this concept is defined *in situ* by the different gurus and teachers who crop up here and there in the epic. Amongst fifty-four occurrences of the word *dharma* in connection with the two almost synonymous adjectives *para* and *parama* (supreme), and dealing with about thirty different topics (notably, truth, non-violence, the contents of the *Veda*, engendering, and respect for the guru), Hiltebeitel shows that the notion of non-cruelty, *ānṛśaṃsya*, mentioned eight times, stands out from all the others. Non-violence, *ahiṃsā*, or more precisely according to its etymology, the non-desire to kill (mentioned four times in this list), is of course an ideal. But in the context of the war this ideal has to be well understood. One does not kill for the sake of killing, in the same way that, according to the Vedic principle, 'to kill in a sacrifice is not killing' (*Laws of Manu*, 5, 39). One acts on another level where the inevitable violence of the conflict is attenuated and rendered acceptable by non-cruelty, which is a form of detachment. And Yudhiṣṭhira, to whom these teachings are foremost addressed, applies this principle in numerous circumstances even outside of the war properly so-called. What is more, in the final episode of the epic, where he refuses to abandon the dog who accompanies him, the *dharmarājan* demonstrates an even greater virtue, compassion, *anukrośa*.[7]

The Buddhist ideal of renunciation is thus not swept away in this new perspective which takes as its normative example the duties of a *kṣatriya*. It becomes, in conformity with the teachings of the *Bhagavad-gītā*, an interior abandonment, a non-attachment to the fruits of one's acts, a perfect detachment, which is the only guarantee of obtaining deliverance and liberation from the cycle of rebirth. The ritual act, now far less formalised than in the Vedic world, is transformed, in the way of *bhakti*, into devotion to the supreme divinity advocated for the whole of society, and thus open to all castes. As Biardeau concludes,

> All Hindus know, at least implicitly, that while officially relying on the *Veda*, in keeping it as the supreme point of reference, the Mbh is in fact

[7] The difference between this word and *ānṛśaṃsya* or *ahiṃsā*, is that the word *anukrośa* does not contain a privative *a-*. It is the state of feeling sorrow 'for' or 'in the place of' (*anu*) another.

the founding charter of what in India is called the religion of *bhakti*, devotion, and that the Vedic texts lend themselves with difficulty to this new reading. Not only is what was scattered and disjointed firmly established within a complex plot, but the overall system is new, radically new, as we pass from a sacrifice centred on the expectation of some gain, to the complete abandonment of self into the hands of a supreme divinity, Viṣṇu, incarnated in Kṛṣṇa, and that all this is addressed, above all, to the *kṣatriya* (1985: 1, 28).

From the traditional point of view, this aspect of things finds its confirmation in the name of the eponymous king of India whose descendants live out the conflict of Kurukṣetra. Indeed, the name Bharata, derived, as we have seen, from the root *BHṚ*, to bear or support, is above all a name of Agni, Fire, being that which must be supported, that is, maintained by men, and which thus plays an essential role in conveying the sacrifice in 'the heat of battle'. The *Mahābhārata* is not only *The Great War of the Descendants of Bharata* or *The Work of Great Weight*; it is also *The Great Sacrifice of the Devotees of Agni*.

What is more, in the *Bhagavad-gītā*, the battlefield, the *kṣetra*, is explicitly likened to the body (*śarīra*). Kṛṣṇa says: 'This *kṣetra* is made up, briefly, of [five] great subtle elements, the ego, the intelligence, the undifferentiated, the ten senses, the inner sense and the five objects of the senses.[8] It is desire, hatred, pleasure, happiness, pain,

8 The twenty-four elements enumerated here become the twenty-four principles of *Sāṃkhya*, to which can be added, in-

the [bodily] aggregate, thought and will' (13, 5–6). This for the devotee of Kṛṣṇa is, as it is for all spiritual men, the real battlefield, and his fight, his effort to overcome himself, is what the Muslim tradition calls so eloquently the *jihād al-akbar*, the greater holy war. One also sees that if the great examples of behaviour found in the *Mahābhārata* are provided by the two highest castes in the Brahmanic hierarchy, this does not at all mean the other classes are excluded. It is in fact a common feature of all legends—and countless examples can be found all over the world—that it is more or less automatic for the reader or listener, no matter how humble his social status, to identify with the kings and princes in the story. The primordial man, *puruṣa*, in the famous Vedic hymn (*Ṛg-veda*, 10, 90), who dismembers himself in an auto-sacrifice, symbolises not only a perfect concordance with the macrocosm, the universe, and the microcosm, man, but also with what unites the two entities in a 'mesocosm', that is, a human society; the mouth of *puruṣa*, or, by synecdoche, his face, becomes the priest, the Brahmin; his arms the warrior, the *kṣatriya*; his thighs the wealthy people, the *vaiśya*; and his feet the servants, the *śūdra*. Just as the universe is an image of man, society is necessarily so also. One might add that in this global vision, the first two castes which are endowed with the spiritual authority and the temporal power, essentially correspond to the two deiform faculties of man which are his intelligence and his will, and that the emphasis put on

dependently of them, the *puruṣa*, in twenty-fifth position. The undifferentiated or non-developed is *prakṛti*, who is not produced at all but produces the twenty-three other principles. On all this we refer to Guénon (2001) and to the*Sāṃkhya-kārikā*.

this ruling part of society is sufficiently justified by the symbolism. But the *śūdra* also has a head and arms and, in this sense, 'the reader's guide to the education of the Dharma king [Yudhiṣṭhira],' as Hiltebeitel describes the *Mahābhārata*, concerns everyone as well as the potential king, which is why the epic is so popular at all levels of society. In a totally different context, namely a play about a king by Shakespeare (*Henry IV*), Martin Lings explains that '... it must be remembered that in the world of Plato and St Augustine no man who was less than a saint could possibly pass as "the ideal king"' (1996: 15). We can deduce the following corollary, that sanctity is a truly initiatic royal way. It is open to all, and he who has achieved the goal, whatever his caste, can be told like Dante through the voice of Virgil: *Lo tuo piacere omai prendi per duce... per ch'io te sovra te corono e mitrio* ('From now on take your pleasure as your guide ... over yourself I crown and mitre you,' trans. Dr Robert Hollander).[9]

[9] Dante, *Purgatory*, 27: 131 and 142, cited by Coomaraswamy (1971: 23).

9

The Symbolism of the Chariot

THE *BHAGAVAD-GĪTĀ* has sometimes been described as a 'moral lesson on action', a tautology which may be considered accurate if it is understood that the 'morality' in question is defined by the notion of *dharma* and its opposite, *adharma*. The fundamental categories of Christian doctrine, which are good and evil, that Dumézil referred to (ch. 5), are thus relativised to the extent, at least, that what is good for one individual is not necessarily so for another. Each person must in fact obey *sva-dharma*, his personal *dharma*, defined by his caste, sex, age, profession, family situation, etc., and this principle precedes all others: 'Better to accomplish one's own *dharma* though without merit, than perfectly that of another. He who does what he must do according to his own nature incurs no sin' (18, 47).[1]

In the *Bhagavad-gītā* this moral teaching is given by Kṛṣṇa in his role as charioteer to Arjuna, the warrior

[1] The same verse appears also in 3, 35, with a variation in the second half: 'To die while accomplishing his own duty is preferable to jeopardising himself by accomplishing another's.'

who will become the perfect devotee and the model of disinterested action. Now, the symbolism of the chariot is interpreted elsewhere in a different way to the one we just saw, when Duryodhana said that the chariot was the altar of the sacrifice. In a famous dialogue retold in an early *Upaniṣad*, the god Yama (Death) meets a young Brahmin named Naciketas to whom he delivers a teaching. He says:

> Know [O Naciketas], the *ātman* to be the master of the chariot, the body to be the chariot. Know also the intelligence (*buddhi*) to be the charioteer, and the reason (*manas*) the reins.
>
> The senses they call the horses, the objects of the senses their roads. Wise people call 'the Enjoyer' (*bhoktṛ*) this coupling of the *ātman*, the senses and reason.[2]
>
> He whose reason is not yoked and whose senses are not under control has no discernment and he is like the charioteer of unmanageable horses.
>
> But he whose reason is always yoked acquires discernment. His senses are under control like the docile horses of a charioteer.
>
> He who has no discernment, who acts unmindfully, remains always impure. He does not attain

---

2 The coupling of the *ātman*, the senses and reason is, significantly, described by a neutral word, *yukta*, from the same root as *yoga*. Prior to the discipline of spiritual union, *yoga* is, properly speaking, the yoke to which oxen and horses are coupled. The *ṛṣi* Pratikṣatra declared: 'Like a horse who knows, I have coupled myself to the yoke' (*Ṛg-veda*, 5, 46, 1).

the supreme goal but remains subject to the changing world (*saṃsāra*).

But he who exercises discernment and controls his mind is always pure. He reaches the supreme goal which releases him from all (transitory) rebirth.

The man who has for charioteer discernment controlling the reins of the mind, reaches the end of the journey, which is the supreme abode of Viṣṇu (*Kathopaniṣad* 3, 3–9).

We wish to stress here, first of all, the allusion in this text to Viṣṇu, who takes the place here, according to all appearances, of *brahman*, the supreme Reality, the Absolute. The *Kathopaniṣad*, even if it predates the epic and belongs by definition to the Vedic corpus, seems to herald or foreshadow the Vaisnavite current and the *bhakti* which is its most essential feature. Then it is important not to confuse the concepts of *buddhi* and *manas*, which more than one translation of Indian texts has rendered too vaguely. We have translated it here as intelligence and reason. The first of these faculties is transcendent in relation to the second. One can also say that the intelligence is situated on the vertical plane while the reason operates on the horizontal plane, or again, that the intelligence has its seat in the heart and the reason in the forehead. The *buddhi*, the intelligence or the intellect, is the place of choices (*inter-legere*, to choose between), that is to say, the free will that enables a man to participate in the divine and to give the human condition its full value. *Manas*, reason, acts, on the other hand, on the plane of the mind[3] in conjunction with the information which the five senses provide. This is why *manas* is sometimes described as a sixth sense or the inward sense. Thus there is no shortage of men with a great capacity for reasoning, but whose cardiac intelligence remains atrophied, whereas there are others, saints notably, who are supremely intelligent while being very limited at combinatorial reasoning. He who reasons without intelligence is no longer master of the direction in which he moves, and it is the horses, symbolised by the senses, which lead him to their own liking. Incidentally, it is precisely in its symbolic meaning, and not in its practical use, that it is said that the horse is the greatest conquest ever made by man. So, in choosing the avatar as his charioteer, that is to say, pure intelligence, Arjuna is saved because his action is right even if he does die in the battle that lies ahead. And it is he and not Kṛṣṇa who must fight, or rather act, and not wallow in inaction, as we have just seen above. It is the same as when Saint Paul declares: 'I live, yet not I, but Christ liveth in me' (Gal. 2: 20). As for Kṛṣṇa, he is confined in this situation to the role of guide, in virtue of the pact he made with his companion at the time of his rallying to the Pāṇḍava cause.

We have seen above (ch. 3) that Kṛṣṇa and Arjuna on their common chariot are called the two Kṛṣṇa (*kṛṣṇau*), the two black fighters. It is impossible to stress enough the strength of the bond that unites them and which makes the Pāṇḍava the avatar's *alter ego*. Arjuna and

---

3 The word *manas*, derived from the root *MAN*, to think, is related to the Latin *mens*, to which is connected the word mind, amongst others.

Kṛṣṇa, whom one must mention here in that order, are in reality incarnations of two particularly venerated *ṛṣi*, Nara and Nārāyaṇa, whose names are generally joined. In the epic, Nara, the man, is Arjuna, and Nārāyaṇa[4] is Kṛṣṇa. It is the elder Bhīṣma who reveals this identity to Duryodhana and his companions on the battlefield:

> See these two heroes, the two warriors Vāsudeva[5] and Arjuna, mounted together on their chariot. They are, says Revelation, the gods of the origin, Nara and Nārāyaṇa, invincible in the world of men, and even to the gods and demons and their kings. Kṛṣṇa is Nārāyaṇa, Phālguna [Arjuna] is Nara, Tradition says. Nārāyaṇa and Nara are one and the same being divided in two. Both have acquired by their actions the imperishable worlds forever. They are born now here, now there, wherever there is war (cf. Biardeau, 2002: 1, 142–3).

Nārāyaṇa is one of the best-known names of Viṣṇu, who is called thus when he is represented sleeping and dreaming on the serpent Śeṣa, reclining on the sea of milk between two cosmic creations. But in this context

---

4 *Nara* means quite simply the Man. While Nārāyaṇa is 'He who is a way (*ayana*) for man' or, according to hermeneutics, 'He who is lying on the waters.' We have seen (ch. 3) that Nārāyaṇa is also reborn as Vyāsa.

5 Vāsudeva, the son of Vasudeva (the long first 'a' indicates a derivation), is a patronymic for Kṛṣṇa. The adjective *vasu*, substantivized, describes a class of gods. It means good, benevolent or shining, and Vasudeva is etymologically the celestial being (*deva*) who is beneficent or shining.

it refers, according to Biardeau, to a celebrated hymn in the *Ṛg-veda* (10, 90) where he is identified as Puruṣa, the primordial man who creates the world through his auto-sacrifice. His association with Nara recalls another hymn in the *Ṛg-veda* (1, 164, 20) where it is said: 'Two birds, a pair of friends, perch on the same tree. One eats the sweet fig of the pipal, while the other, without eating, watches him' (Biardeau's translation). Now, this image runs through the corpus of *śruti*, since it can be found as such in two important *Upaniṣad*, the *Muṇḍaka* (3, 1) and the *Śvetāśvatara* (4, 6). It represents contemplation and action, and we will discuss this theme further on. Biardeau concludes: 'The epic certainly has the image of the two birds in mind when it talks about Nara and Nārāyaṇa, and this also goes for Arjuna and Kṛṣṇa as they are two "descents" on earth of the two *ṛṣi*' (*ibid.*). In other words, Arjuna and Kṛṣṇa symbolise what is sometimes called the I and the Self, the outward man and the inward man.

Leaving aside now the strict framework of the symbolism of the chariot, let us pause for a moment on another association with the two Kṛṣṇa, equally rich in significance. We have seen in chapter 3 that Draupadī, daughter of Drupada, is actually called Kṛṣṇā, the Black One. She thus shares with her husband, Arjuna, the honour of bearing the same name as the avatar, and her role as perfect *bhaktā* is clearly revealed in the dice game, which causes the temporary destruction of the Pāṇḍava clan. On the point of being stripped naked, the princess has, in fact, the 'good sense' to invoke the help of the avatar. She does this inwardly, as he is physically absent from the scene. Now, this inward prayer shows the normal relationship between *buddhi*, *manas* and the five senses. Kṛṣṇa is the *buddhi*; Draupadī, the *manas*; and her five husbands are the five senses. The episode of the endless sari bears witness, in its way, to the pertinence of the exegesis which affirms that the marriage of *manas* and the five senses is also symbolised by the polyandrous union of Draupadī and her five husbands:[6] in turning to and trusting in the pure *buddhi* in these tragic circumstances, the *manas* avoids the 'dismemberment' of the brotherhood of the five senses. We saw above (ch. 5) that Śrī, in the form of Draupadī, was not the consort of the incarnation of Viṣṇu, but that she contracted a quintuple union with Indra, and that this apparent anomaly puzzled Dumézil. The interpretation we have given here seems to offer a solution to this enigma, and we have as possible proof the Sanskrit word for the senses which is *indriya*, literally that which is related to Indra. Finally, the rescue of Draupadī beautifully illustrates the fact that reason (*manas*) can be illuminated by the intelligence (*buddhi*), because having been delivered from this humiliation, the young wife of the Pāṇḍava finds the inspiration which allows her to challenge the validity of the game of dice by arguing that Yudhiṣṭhira was not entitled to bet her, having lost himself before: a slave who is not master of himself is even less, *a fortiori*, the master of his wife.

To conclude this chapter, mention should be made of the fact that the symbolism of the chariot appears under many guises in the Western tradition, starting in the Bible with the case of Elias's ascent into Heaven in a chariot of fire. But it is in Plato's *Phaedrus* (246) that

---

[6] We will come back to this point in chapter 13.

one finds the most interesting parallel to the chariot in the *Kathopaniṣad*. The basic idea is the same, but it is exploited differently: Socrates judges in fact that while the gods are quite capable of guiding their chariots, men are faced with the challenge of having to direct both a well-trained and a badly-trained horse at the same time. What is important to note here is the universality of the symbolism, notwithstanding the interpretation determined by a given context: the question is not whether the Indians borrowed this symbol from Greece as some Orientalists have supposed, but to be aware that in the traditional world a symbolic reading of myths and legends goes without saying. And, in this way, the train of thought offered by the author of the *Kathopaniṣad* undeniably constitutes an important key to the reading of the *Mahābhārata*.

10

The Doctrine of the Four Ages

THE BATTLE OF Kurukṣetra, like any universal war, is a crisis in the full sense of being a divine judgement. It therefore implies an eschatological concern that crystallised in the doctrine of the four ages of the world, and which would undergo considerable developments in all the Puranic literature. This new concept of time, which the *Mānavadharmaśāstra*, *The Laws of Manu*, also refers to, and which became a cornerstone of Hinduism, divides the history of the world into four periods (*yuga*) of shortening duration, which correspond, as we have seen, to the four ages symbolised by metals in the Greek tradition. However, the Indians do not make any reference to metals. They name these ages: the *kṛta-yuga*, or perfect age; the *tretā-yuga*, the age indicated by the number 3; the *dvāpara-yuga*, the age indicated by the number 2; and the *kali-yuga*, the age indicated by the number 1. Essentially, from a spiritual point of view, the conditions of life degenerate over the course of this 'evolution' which ends in a catastrophe, a dissolution (*pralaya*), before the cycle can begin again, and so on, indefinitely.[1] The series 4, 3, 2, 1, which totals 10, shows the respective duration of each age, the first one lasting four times longer than the last. As the war in the *Mahābhārata* inaugurates the *kali-yuga*, we now live in the dark age, awaiting the dissolution. In addition, the shortening of the length of time of the ages manifests the principle of a progressive acceleration of the decadence of the world, of which the contemporary age, with its cult of speed and technological innovation, provides a striking image for the Hindu collective imagination.[2]

In relation to the length of the ages, *The Laws of Manu* (1, 67f.) give the following numbers: the *kṛta-yuga* lasts 4,000 years, preceded and followed by two twilight eras (*saṃdhi*) of two hundred years each, which makes a total of 4,400 years; then, by a declining calculation, one obtains, including the twilight eras, 3,600 years for the *tretā-yuga*, 2,400 for the *dvāpara-yuga* and 1,200 for the *kali-yuga*, which makes a total of 12,000 years. It is possible that these lengths of duration were at first taken literally, but that later they were deemed too short and were then lengthened artificially. This is more or less what occurs in the Judaeo-Christian tradition where Peter says: 'Be not ignorant of this one thing, that one day is with the Lord as a thousand years, and a thousand years as one day' (II Peter 3: 8, recalling Psalms 90: 4). Still, *The*

---

1 'Belief in the periodic creation and destruction of the Universe is found as early as in the *Atharva Veda* (X, 8, 39–40), and as a matter of fact it belongs to the *Weltanschauung* of all archaic societies' (Mircea Eliade, 1961: 62).

2 For a complete description of this doctrine, we refer the reader to Luis González-Reimann (2002).

Laws of Manu offer the following equation: 'A year for mortals is a day and night of the gods; and this is how it is divided: the day corresponds to the northern course of the sun and the night to its southern course.' Therefore, the preceding numbers must be multiplied by 360 in order to find the real duration of the ages given above to make the 'divine' years into their equivalent ordinary years. Thus we get the number 4,320,000 years for the whole cycle and 432,000 for the *kali-yuga* alone, numbers that are generally found in the Puranic literature.

Orientalists have pointed out, quite rightly, that the 'theory' of the four ages, as Dumézil calls it, is not to be found anywhere in Vedic literature, which, this author adds, does not mean it did not exist at a very early date in the Aryan tradition. The French scholar comes up with several conjectures as to why this should be the case, questioning the Indo-European sources in an attempt to shed light on its emergence in the *Mahābhārata*. But, quite curiously, he does not say anything in the pages of *Mythe et épopée* that he dedicates to this subject (1, 218ff.), on the convergence that we have just pointed out between the Indian and the Homeric tradition; he limits his comparisons to Iranian and Scandinavian eschatology. However, be that as it may, it is time to show that one can equally find traces of similar myths other than in the Indo-European world. There is, first of all, in the Bible the strange case of the colossus with feet of clay in Nebuchadnezzar's vision interpreted by the prophet Daniel (Daniel, 2). The giant statue seen by the king of Babylon had a golden head, a silver chest and arms, a stomach and thighs of bronze, legs of iron, and the feet were a mixture of clay and iron which made them very fragile. In addition to matching the four metals that the Greeks attributed to the four successive ages of the decline of the world perfectly, the different parts of the statue are exactly the same, with the exception of the particular detail concerning the feet, as those of the Vedic Puruṣa that we have already encountered (ch. 8). These coincidences reinforce, in an unexpected way, the connection between the four ages and the four castes that the Indian tradition makes. What is more, Daniel gives this vision an essentially historical explanation that is linked to time, alluding to the immediate demise of Nebuchadnezzar's kingdom. He teaches in this way the impermanence of all human glory and achievement. For their part, Christians also express the same idea, but on a vaster scale, likening the stone thrown at the statue, and which made it topple over, to Christ himself, called upon to reverse the degeneration of the world as a result of the fall. They also connect this stone with the one rejected by the builders which became the chief cornerstone (Luke 20:17, referring to Psalms 118:22).

But there is something even more interesting. The Indian tradition compares the world to a bull (*e.g.*: *Mānavadharmaśāstra*, 1, 8, or *Mahābhārata*, 3, 190, 9–10); the bull of *dharma*, which, in the first age, stands firmly on its four legs. But in each transition from one age to another it loses a leg, and in the present age, the *kali-yuga*, it stands precariously on one teetering leg.[3] This

---

[3] The number 4 plays a particularly important role in the Hindu world. It can be found in the four *Veda*, the four ages of the world, the four goals in life (*puruṣārtha*), the four stages in man's life (*āśrama*), the four socio-religious castes (*varṇa*), the four requirements for being a Hindu (to acknowledge the

means that today only a quarter of the original *dharma* is still respected. Now, this bull has an exact equivalent in the Amerindian world with the buffalo in the tradition of the Sioux Lakota as described by Héhaka Sapa (Black Elk). Allow us to quote at some length the commentary by Joseph Epes Brown, who recorded the words of this great sage.

> The buffalo was to the Sioux the most important of all four-legged animals, for it supplied their food, their clothing and even their houses which were made from the tanned hides. Because the buffalo contained all these things within himself, and for many other reasons, he was a natural symbol of the universe, the totality of all manifested forms. Everything is symbolically contained within this animal. The earth and all that grows from her, all animals and even the two-legged peoples; and each specific part of the beast represents for the Indians one of these 'parts' of creation. Also the buffalo has four legs and these represent the four ages which are an integral condition of creation.

And:

> According to Sioux mythology, it is believed that at the beginning of the cycle a buffalo was placed

---

sanctity of the *Veda*, to belong to a caste, to worship an image of god and to venerate the cow), the four great gods, (Brahmā, Viṣṇu, Śiva and the Devī), the four states of the *ātman*, the four heads and the four sons of Brahmā, the four oceans that encompass the earth, the four arms and the four weapons of Viṣṇu, etc.

> at the west to hold back the waters. Every year this buffalo loses one hair and every age he loses one leg. When all his hair and all his legs have gone the waters rush in once again and the cycle comes to an end.... It is believed by both the American Indian and the Hindu that at the present time the buffalo or bull is on his last leg and he is very nearly bald. Corresponding beliefs could be cited from many other traditions (Héhaka Sapa, 1971: 6, n. 8; 9, n. 15).

The problems posed by this symbolic enigma to those scholars who are eager to explain everything by borrowings and who are engaged in a systematic hunt for common sources appears here rather difficult! However, in the Eurasian world, one can assume a common Babylonian heritage for Indo-European and Semitic peoples.

For man, a measure of time that is cyclic and not linear is natural, because duration is only perceptible to common experience thanks to the cosmic cycles, from the alternation of day and night to the precession of the equinoxes, passing through those intermediate phases which are the monthly cycles dependent on the moon and the yearly cycles dependent on the sun. The opposite idea of a linear time, with all the notion of progress it implies, is also legitimate, of course, but only within a framework which, in the traditional view, must be necessarily subordinate to the preceding conception. Human life remains the absolute paradigm of our concept of time, and for all traditions the microcosmic cycle of dust to dust is that of the eternal return. The history of the world is thus a reflection of our life,[4] with the notion that the time when we still have a choice is dwindling by the hour, and that once the innocence of childhood has been lost, the need to 'outwit time' (*kāla-vañcana*, the expression is borrowed from Tantrism) to gain eternity becomes increasingly urgent. The risk of wasting the human state through a lack of control over the reins increases with each moment, and as Saint Francis has said: 'Woe to those who die in mortal sin' ('*guai a'cquelli ke morrano ne le peccata mortali*'; *Canticle of the Creatures*, 29).

We know that, unlike in Greece, which is silent on this point, the succession of the four ages, or *yuga*, in the Puranic tradition fits into the rhythm of ever vaster cycles: the *mahāyuga*; the *manvantara*; then the *kalpa*, or days of Brahmā, which themselves compose, in their turn, the years of Brahmā; then the lives of Brahmā, and so on *ad libitum*. We have discussed elsewhere the different cosmic cycles in relation to the concomitant notion of the co-eternity of manifestation,[5] and we will not return to it here. In contrast, we would like to add a few thoughts on the way in which this doctrine is sometimes perceived in present day India. In the chapter of his book dedicated to the *yuga* in the epic (2010: 180–

---

4 The word which designates the world in the Germanic languages, *Welt* (Ger.) or world (Eng.), comes from Indo-European (via ancient German) **wer-***aldh*. The element **wer* corresponds to the Latin *vir* and the element **aldh* to the German *alt* and the English old. The world is thus 'the age of man,' or, as is said in Sanskrit, a *manvantara*, an age of Manu. The equation macrocosm/microcosm is eloquently expressed in the etymology of this key notion.

5 Cf. *The Queen and the Avatar*, pp. 93, 115.

201), the Indologist González-Reimann surveys modern conceptions on this subject, and the least one can say is that the greatest confusion reigns. It should be noted that we are here at the intersection, both scabrous and delicate, between the strict tenets of traditional India and the influences of various Western occultists. The latter have played a role that is far from negligible in the reflections of more than one school of thought in present day Hinduism, from the founder of the Arya Samaj, Dayananda Sarasvati (1824–1883), to the creator of the International Society for Krishna Consciousness, Swami Prabhupāda (A.C. Bhaktivedanta, 1896–1977), and including, among others, Vivekananda (1863–1902) and Aurobindo Ghose (1872–1950), each one adding his say, with significant differences, however. The common preoccupation of all these people is to date as precisely as possible the *kali-yuga* in relation to the present day. In other words, to interpret symbols in a historical way, which no doubt is a 'sign of the times'.

Amongst all these assorted efforts, there is one that really does not seem to interest González-Reimann at all and which he promptly relegates to the dustbin of occultism. If in the traditional worlds one always does without dogmas of this type, and even if it cannot claim to be anything more than one hypothesis among others, it still merits special attention. We are referring here to René Guénon's thesis which in 'Some Remarks on the Doctrine of the Cosmic Cycles' (1970), an article originally published in 1937, offers an interesting perspective on the subject. The French metaphysician starts with two assumptions: the first is that the number of 432,000 solar years, which the *Purāṇa* generally gives for the duration of the *kali-yuga* and which represents a tenth of the complete length of a *manvantara*[6] or era of Manu, was artificially multiplied by 100 with the intent to mislead people who might misuse it for making predictions, and that in fact only the first four digits should be retained, thus bringing the length of time in question to 4,320 years;[7] the second is that this number is closely linked to that of the precession of the equinoxes, traditionally estimated as being 25,920 years, since 4,320 × 6 = 25,920.[8] Considering that half of this number makes 12,960 years, which corresponds to 'the great year' of the Persians and the Greeks, Guénon concludes that the number of a *manvantara* must include an integer of these 'great years'. Now, 'with the Chaldeans, the duration of Xisuthros' reign, who is obviously identical to Vaivaswata, the Manu of the present era, is set at 64,800 years, which is exactly five "great years"' (*ibid.*, 23). The number 5 being that of the *bhūta*, the elements of the sensible world, it seems

---

6 Guénon has been justly criticised for referring to a little known definition of the *manvantara* which creates confusion between it and a *mahāyuga*, the usual word to designate a cycle made up of 4 ages. According to the *Mānavadharmaśāstra* and various *Purāṇa*, in fact, 71 *mahāyuga* make up one *manvantara*. Beyond that, 14 of these *manvantara* make up a day of Brahmā, and we are now in the 7th of the present series, but this does not invalidate the rigour of Guénon's calculations.

7 This represents an average in relation to the equation between divine years and human years formulated in the *Laws of Manu*. It should be noted that this equation is not always applied in traditional Hindu texts.

8 A quick look at a dozen astronomical encyclopedias and Internet sites shows that this length of time, always given approximately, is between 25,700 and 26,000 years long.

to be naturally connected to a cosmological perspective. And as 4,320 years represents a third of the great year, or a fifteenth of 64,800 years, Guénon deduces that this duration should be distributed along the course of a *manvantara* in the following ratios: 2 units for the first age, 1½ for the second, 1 for the third and ½ for the fourth. This comes to a total of 25,920 years for the *kṛta-yuga*, that is, a complete precession of the equinoxes; 19,440 for the *tretā-yuga*; 12,960 for the *dvāpara-yuga*; and 6,480 for the *kali-yuga*. 'And one will own that these numbers are set within perfectly plausible limits and could well correspond to the age of present terrestial humanity' (*ibid.*, 24). Of course, starting with 432,000 and arriving at 6,480 is a mathematical sleight of hand. But, to our knowledge, this calculation is the only one that eloquently expresses the potential of the number 4,320 in an astronomical context. In any case, this number is closely linked to the measurement of a circle, because 4,320 equals 12 × 360. And, as Guénon also notices, it is a multiple of 72 (4,320 = 72 × 60). Now, the movement of the equinoxes is exactly one degree every 72 years, which, says Guénon again, is proof of 'the truly natural character' of the divisions of the circle. What the metaphysician does not take into account, however, is that 72 is also the number of the years of Kṛṣṇa's life, the Kurukṣetra war having taken place halfway through his life during his thirty-sixth year. There is possibly here a connection between the 71 *mahāyuga* needed to make up one *manvantara*: 72 = 71 + 1, the added unit signalling the start of a new cycle or corresponding to a *saṃdhi*, a period of junction between two cycles.

However, Guénon has no intention of attempting to

make a closer calculation as to the exact time of the ending of the present cycle. He concludes:

> We know from all the traditional facts that we have already been in the *Kali-Yuga* for a long time; we can say, with no fear of error, that we are even in a very advanced phase of it, a phase whose descriptions in the Purānas match up besides, in the most striking way, to the characteristics of the present epoch; but would it not be unwise to specify more, and would it not inevitably give rise to the sort of predictions which the traditional doctrine, not without grave reason, opposed so many obstacles to? (*ibid.*, 24).

To which one can add that all traditions see in this incertitude as to the details of these immanent cosmic events an important element of the spiritual condition of man forced as he is to hold onto the outline of the prophecy: 'For ye know neither the day nor the hour,' says Jesus (Matthew, 25:13).[9]

The question that now arises is, why the *yuga* are four in number and not three or five? The solution to this apparent difficulty is to be found in the symbolic relationship that exists between the circle and the square, which already in the most ancient civilisations appeared respectively as Heaven and Earth. Common experience shows the world as a circle or set of circles, whether it be

---

9 However, the *Sūrya-siddhānta*, a treatise on astronomy from the Gupta era (4th century), dates the beginning of the *kali-yuga* to the 18 February 3102 BC, which brings us to 5116 (AD 2014), a date featured on a number of popular Indian calendars.

the arc of the horizon or the orbits of the stars and the planets around the earth. But this circle is not indefinite; it is not without beginning or end. It is 'qualified' by the cardinal directions which, on earth, divide it into four parts. The cross inscribed in the circle is, ultimately, one of the most universal symbols there is. It situates man in the world and determines the fundamental relationship between time and space. In India this symbol serves as the basis of the *svastika* which, depending on the direction of the perpendicular branches of the central cross, indicates either a solar movement (*pradakṣiṇa* = clockwise) or a polar movement (*apradakṣiṇa* = anti-clockwise). The word *svastika* means happiness or well-being, and even if the ritual circumambulations are done in a *pradakṣiṇa* direction in order to keep the center or the object venerated on the right,[10] it is completely erroneous to speak of a good or bad direction with regard to this. It is the same movement seen from two different points of view, like a wheel which turns one way when we look at it from above and another when we look at it from below.

Now, in the traditional perspective the world is often taken as a temple and the temple is taken as a world. In his study on 'The Genesis of the Hindu Temple' (2009: 13–48), Titus Burckhardt builds his reflections quite naturally on the symbolic relationship between the circle and the square. And considering that the square

---

[10] The adjective *dakṣa*, skilled, which is the basis for *pradakṣiṇa*, is also, as a noun, the name of the god of Sacrifice or the Art of ritual. It is related to the Latin *dexter* and the English word dextrous.

of the temple results from the fixation of the principal movements of the heavens, he says:

> The Hindu spirit is in fact always inclined to transpose terrestrial and cosmic realities, divergent though they may be, into the non-separative and static plenitude of the Divine Essence. This spiritual transfiguration in architecture is accompanied by an inversely analogous symbolism, wherein the great 'measures' of time, the various cycles, are 'crystallised' in the fundamental square of the temple (*ibid.*, 15).

This crystallization of the measurement of time in the building of temples can consequently be given different emphases, according to the rite performed for determining the orientation of the temple, by tracing out in the earth a basic square called a *vāstu-puruṣa-maṇḍala*, which can roughly be translated as 'the square of the abode of Man (*puruṣa*)'.[11] There exist 32 types of *vāstu-maṇḍala*, but they can be divided into two main groups, depending on whether the surface thus defined is like a checkerboard or chessboard, and composed

[11] Note that the term *maṇḍala*, which strictly speaking means a circle, has come to mean a square. A famous drawing by Leonardo da Vinci, similar to a *maṇḍala* of this type, represents a man standing both within a square and a circle with his navel at the centre. And Jesus, the Son of Man, crucified at the centre of time and at the centre of the world—commemorated in the layout of the cathedral—also offers a clear image of the identity between the microcosm and the macrocosm. We will recall here that old punishments like crucifixion, impaling and quartering, so cruel and 'barbaric' as they may appear to us, originally had a symbolic significance.

of either four (or a multiple of 4) or 9 (or a multiple of 9) squares. The main difference is that when it is divided by four there is no central square, and when it is divided by nine there is. When there is a central square, the basic *vāstu-maṇḍala* represents the earth (*pṛthivī*); the central square represents the centre of the world, and the eight surrounding squares correspond to the directions of space. In contrast, when starting from a four square model, by circulating round the quaternary, which evokes the seasons and the phases of the moon, one gains an image of time with no other centre than a point representing the eternal present, and the whole square is then the symbol of Śiva, the god of transformation. The nine squared *maṇḍala* (generally extended to 81 squares) is thus not only associated with Viṣṇu, but also the *kṣatriya* caste and the microcosm, whereas the four square *maṇḍala* (generally extended to 64 squares) is associated with Śiva, the Brahmin caste and the macrocosm (*ibid.*, 27–28). In an early work on the symbolism of the Hindu temple, whose authority has not diminished with the passage of time, Stella Kramrisch puts this in perspective along with Guénon's theories that we summarised above. She says:

> All the cyclical numbers in Hindu cosmology are essentially based on the period of the precession of the equinoxes. They are exact fractions of the number 25,920. It is for this reason that the *Vāstumaṇḍala* of the temple, the square diagram of Existence, of time measurable in space, has two main alternative dispositions as far as the metaphysical and cosmological plan of the temple is

concerned. It is laid out either in 64 or else in 81 squares; either number is a sub-multiple of 25,920 which is 64 × 81 × 5. Five is the number of a *Saṃvatsara*, a cycle of 5 lunar-solar years (1976: 36–7).

These considerations, however, call to mind other ideas, and especially this: if the doctrine of the four ages appeared at the same time as the epic and was only made explicit in the *kali-yuga*, one can ask oneself if the man of the *dvāpara-yuga,* which came immediately before, was conscious of the fact that he was in the third age, at an advanced stage of degeneration of the world, but in which many spiritual values were still preserved. It is probably impossible to answer this question in a very satisfactory manner, which presupposes, moreover, that one gives credit to the doctrine of the four ages in the same way that Hindus do. But the *Ṛg-veda*, considered by them to be a relic of this former period, gives us a partial answer. Even though it does not contain eschatological teachings, this collection of hymns is full of allusions to the creation of the world. First, there is the primordial myth of the slaying of the dragon, Vṛtra, by Indra, and then in the last part, the dismemberment of Puruṣa. These two myths introduce the doctrine of the sacrifice. Thus the gaze of the man of the *dvāpara-yuga* was still turned towards the origin, and his religious behaviour was a direct response to the actions of the gods at the beginning. The man of the *kali-yuga*, on the other hand, is definitely in the presence of the approaching end of the *pralaya*, and his spiritual attitude is imbued with the expectancy of a cyclical renewal and the promise of a last intervention by Viṣṇu, who, in the guise of

Kalkyavatāra, will incarnate at the end of the *yuga* with sword drawn and mounted on a white horse. The transition from a ritualism closely connected to a way of works, a *karma-yoga*, which, in retrospect seems rather fussy and demanding, to an acute attention fixed on the signs of the times, coupled with the pending return of a divine incarnation, summarises in the Indian context the religious change linked to the coming of the last age. It is not unlike the main features of the change from its Judaic source to the Christian tradition. The signs of the times which accompany or announce this change form the contents of several lists like the one that the sage Mārkaṇḍeya reveals to Yudhiṣṭhira (3, 190 and the following verses; cf. Biardeau 2002: 1596–99). Included on it is widespread violence, lust, the mixing of the castes, the confusion in the heart of family life, the murderer unpunished, the plundering of widows, the abandonment of the rites, etc.[12] We are on familiar ground here, if one may say so, as a similar rhetoric is common to all the great living religions of the present. No doubt among Hindus faithful to their tradition (whether their sentiments are tainted by the theories of the reformers we have discussed above or not) this discourse resonates and is magnified by the state of the social, religious and ecological tumult of the present day world. And it is said regarding this, that in India today, the superstitious avoid keeping a copy of the *Mahābhārata* in their house for fear of precipitating a disaster.

[12] A list of parallel signs is also given by Bhīṣma in his teaching to Yudhiṣṭhira (12, 69, 92ff.).

Since we have just been considering the evolution of time and the transformation of the cycles, we would like to dedicate a few lines of this chapter to Paule Lerner, who, in a work on the periphery of the huge number of Orientalist offerings (1988), has concentrated on documenting the hypothesis that the *Mahābhārata* is a mythical transposition of the cyclic upheavals accompanying the passage from the age of Aries to the Age of Pisces. We know that this change depends on the movement of the vernal point of the ecliptic on the zodiacal circle due to the precession of the equinoxes. Now, it is possible that at the time the *Mahābhārata* was being composed, India was already aware of this astronomical phenomenon discovered by the Chaldeans,[13] and we have seen the importance that Guénon and Kramrisch place on the cycle which follows it. Even though the shift from one age to another can only be dated approximately, given that the constellations, unlike the signs with the same name, occupy the sky in variable dimensions that have no definite limits, the duration of one age of 2,160 years is nevertheless accurate to the extent that it corresponds to a twelfth of the precession, which is set at 25,920 years. If one takes into account that we, at the beginning of the 21st century, are at the juncture between the Age of Pisces and the Age of Aquarius, we find that the reign of Aśoka, which took place a little over 2,200 years ago, occurred at the dawn of the preceding juncture between the Age of

[13] Although Vedic astronomy was based on a division of the ecliptic into 27 sections or constellations, the *nakṣatra*, and prioritised the observation of the phases of the moon, the Indians adopted Chaldean astronomy as soon as they knew of it, which led to a mixing of the two systems.

Aries and the Age of Pisces.[14] This being the case, it is possible that this subject could have preoccupied the author of the *Mahābhārata*, who could have thus connected the crisis inherent in a cyclic change of this type to that occurring between the belligerents in the war of the Bhārata. Besides, it is a fact that Vedic literature is replete with astronomical allusions showing the interest that this subject had for Indians, indeed to such a degree that among the six traditional sciences consecrated to the interpretation of Scripture, the six *vedāṅga*, astronomy (*jyotiṣa*) holds a prominent place next to phonetics, metrics, lexicology, grammar and the science of ritual performance.

The lunar dynasty represented by Śāntanu, the son of Pratīpa, whose exact name means precession, or retrograde movement, finds itself in deadlock as Bhīṣma, the son of Gaṅgā and the incarnation of the Sky, renounces power and marriage in order to satisfy his father's desire to marry Satyavatī. As the last member of the royal line symbolising the hegemony of Aries, Bhīṣma thus realises, through this voluntary renunciation, the transfer of power. All blood lines are effectively broken between Śāntanu and the putative descendents of the Bhārata, who are in fact the sons of Vyāsa, the secret child of

---

14 For many astrologers, Christianity appears as a religion whose inception coincides with the era of Pisces, and the fact that the fish was one of the first symbols of Christ is for them an unmistakable sign of this providential link. Moreover, Jesus was born of the Virgin Mary, which refers to the opposite and complementary sign of Virgo. The Catholic Church celebrates the Nativity of Mary on the 8th of September, exactly at the middle of the sign of Virgo, a 'coincidence' which we have not seen pointed out anywhere. Is it too obvious?

Satyavatī, herself the daughter of the King of the Fish. It can be added, but here it is Biardeau (2000: 1, 155–157) and not Lerner who points it out, that in the *Sauptika-parvan* it is this same Bhīṣma who teaches Yudhiṣṭhira that the new age is now subject to 'the law of the fish,' *matsyanyāya*, which involves a sort of normalisation of violence, allowing the strong to devour the weak without further ado.

It is impossible to mention here all the proofs that Lerner furnishes from the epic in support of her thesis. If her vast astronomical learning cannot be denied, either on the modern scientific level or on the traditional plane, she can however be criticised in a general way for the fact that the references to obvious astronomical facts, and those dependent on a very tenuous speculation, are not often sufficiently distinguished. The reader is thus inundated with correspondences which are often difficult to connect to each other, and one cannot help but feel here, that the best is the enemy of the good, and that Paule Lerner has probably stretched things a little in order to build up her argument. As the studies of Dumézil, Biardeau, Hiltebeitel and, *a fortiori*, the diverse traditional points of view we have examined, reveal, Vyāsa is anything but just an astrology monomaniac. That said, the criticism of a book like *Astrological Key of the Mahābhārata* presupposes a vast erudition in both astronomy and Indology, two sciences rarely found in the same scholar. One may have to wait a long time before someone emerges who can clarify and refine its contents, unless Hiltebeitel's final judgement has not definitively stopped in their tracks any further enterprises of this sort.[15] It seemed worth lingering on this thesis, for it eminently shows, in our eyes, the multiplicity of interpretations that can be spawned by such a complex and sophisticated work as the *Mahābhārata*.

15 'Lerner's "astrological key", as an allegory of a shift related to the precession of the equinoxes by a process of Jungian psychic integration, seems far more superimposed on the *Mbh* than elicited from the text' (2001: 9).

11

The Dice Game and the King's Destiny

One of the most dramatic moments in the epic is, without doubt, the two games of dice which result in the temporary defeat of the Pāṇḍava and their subsequent exile to the forest for twelve years, followed by a thirteenth year hiding incognito in the kingdom of Virāṭa. Let us recall that Duryodhana, driven on by his desire to ruin his cousins and wrest from them their share of the kingdom, thinks up the trap of inviting Yudhiṣṭhira, who is well known for his passion for dice, to a 'friendly' game in order to divest him of everything he owns. He is sure of his plan thanks to the help of his evil genius, his maternal uncle Śakuni, the Bird (of evil omen), who is a notorious cheater and who plays on his behalf. However, he needs to do this twice, for after the first game, when Yudhiṣṭhira has lost everything including his brothers, himself and his wife, the latter—we have referred more than once to this scene—in a last-ditch attempt to overcome Duryodhana's treachery, claims that her husband was not entitled to bet her, as he had already lost himself. But after the reprieve *in extremis* of the five Pāṇḍava and their wife, the relentless Kaurava manages to convince his father, King Dhṛtarāṣṭra, to allow them to play a second game. In spite of the horrified protests of the queen and the elders of the court, the blind old man, who is well-known for his weak character, finally gives in, as he always does on the insistence of his son, and Yudhiṣṭhira, who cannot withdraw from the game, loses once again and is forced to flee to the forest with his brothers and his wife.

We saw above (ch. 6) that playing dice is a favourite 'past-time' of Śiva's, but that this game is strongly condemned by Kṛṣṇa because it is closely connected to the corrosive nature of time, and this is evident in the very shape of the dice. In India, in fact, these are made of sections of a square rule. As a result, only four sides come into play, and it is their four numerical values which give rise, in descending order, to the names of the four ages that we discussed in the preceding chapter. Now Duryodhana and Śakuni are, in reality, demons, *asura*, and they incarnate respectively *kali* and *dvāpara*, the numbers one and two, the worst possible throws corresponding to the last two ages. In playing against them, Yudhiṣṭhira, the son of Dharma, can only lose, at least temporarily, in giving way to the corrosive logic of the degenerating world. The fact that in the fateful game it is Śakuni, a notorious cheater, who takes the place of his nephew, shows in sum that the seed of the *kali-yuga* was already germinating in the preceding age: Śakuni carries within himself the destructive virus of duplicity which is only found occasionally in the age he represents; his success sanctions it and makes it a hallmark of the constituent conflicts of the new world to which he gives birth.

That the game of dice is specifically an activity of the gods is, what is more, inscribed in etymology. The root *DIV* to which the word *deva*, the equivalent in Sanskrit of the Latin *deus*, is related, means, first of all, to shine (in the sky). But it also has a second well-known meaning, which is to cast the dice.[1] The term *daiva*, literally 'that which is relative to *deva*', properly refers to fate with all the consequences that come with the ineluctable verdict of a roll of the dice. Hence, the ungovernable passion for dice that grips Yudhiṣṭhira, a passion that at first sight seems strange in a man who is an ideal king in so many ways, takes on a new significance, for this passion is a Passion. The son of Dharma conforms to a logic that is strictly connected to the reality he incarnates, submission to the trials of an inevitable degradation over the course of time. For such is his fate: the bull of *dharma* must 'lose a leg' at each change from age to age, and the Passion of Yudhiṣṭhira who, on the earthly plane, is inescapably doomed to lose all his possessions in a game of dice and be exiled, is that of *dharma*, powerless to avoid its cyclical erosion before the return of a new golden age. Since we are speaking of the Passion, it is somewhat tempting in the present context to recall here that when Christ hung naked on the cross, his tunic, representing the outer garment of society, was coveted by four soldiers, precisely, who cast lots for it so that it would not have to be divided.

---

[1] See, regarding this etymology, *The Queen and the Avatar* (p. 46–47), where we also developed the idea that chance is a metaphor for the divine, where the actions of the gods appear seemingly random in the eyes of men who cannot perceive their intrinsic logic.

If in Indian civilisation it is the priests who, as 'specialists' of the sacred and guardians of the doctrine, are the holders of spiritual authority, the temporal power legitimately belongs to the king, who is the supreme head of the *kṣatriya* caste. The relationship governing priesthood and kingship has its prototype in the relations in the Vedic context, on the one hand between Mitra and Varuṇa, and on the other between Agni and Indra.[2] In this relationship, the second must always be subordinate to the first, at the risk of society coming adrift. It is thus that:

> ... already in RV.VIII.100.1, Indra is manifestly Agni's *bhakta*, and this is the natural relation of the *Regnum* to the *Sacerdotium*; and in RV.X.51.8 those whom Agni calls upon to 'give my share' (*data bhāgam*) are to be his *bhaktas*. Every sacrifice involves the giving of the share (*bhāgam*) that is due to the recipient, and is in this sense a devotion, ultimately of the sacrificer himself, the devotee; this implies love, because love is the cause of all giving, but it remains that *bhakti* can be more literally translated by 'participation' in some contexts and by 'devotion' in others, than by 'love', for which the word is *prema*... (Coomaraswamy, 1999: footnote 140).

Now, in the epic, 'Krishna and Arjuna are to be identified with the mythical Agni and Indra' (*ibid.*, 5). This quotation from Coomaraswamy shows, incidentally, where

2 On all this, see Coomaraswamy (1978). In contrast to Dumézil (cf. ch. 5), Coomaraswamy gives numerous irrefutable arguments for explicitly allying Varuṇa to the second function.

one should look in the Vedic literature for the roots of *bhakti*. It also shows that the king, as an agent of the sacrifice, who must renew it ceaselessly, has his role inscribed in time. If the spiritual authority is in direct contact with the eternal, the temporal power—and this is a truism which is sometimes forgotten—is in direct contact with time, and here there is an inverse analogy to what was said above concerning the structure of temples. In the Śaivite temple of sixty-four squares representing time, the Brahmin presides over the immutable, and in the Vaisnavite temple of eighty-one squares representing space, the *kṣatriya* commands becoming.

In his famous speech to Yudhiṣṭhira, Bhīṣma, on his bed of arrows, explains this in detail to his great-nephew:

> Do not question whether it is Time which makes a king or the king who makes Time. When the king correctly and completely applies the rules of punishment (*daṇḍanīti*), then a Kṛtayuga has been set in motion by Time. During this Kṛtayuga, only *dharma* exists, and there is no *adharma* at all; in none of the *varṇa* do the people take pleasure in *adharma* [...] When the king only applies three-quarters of the rules of administering punishment and lets drop the last quarter, the Tretā has been inaugurated and a quarter of ill fortune accompanies the other three quarters. The earth with all its plants only bears fruit when it is cultivated. [Here follow the corresponding descriptions of the other two ages followed by the conclusion:] The king is the creator of the Kṛta, Tretā and Dvā-

parayuga, the king is also the cause of the fourth age.

The passage concludes by enumerating the rewards conferred on the king who gains heaven by creating the *kṛta-yuga*, the mixed rewards for creating the middle two ages, and hell for producing the *kali-yuga* (Biardeau's translation, 2002: 1, 154–5).

What does 'the king shapes the times' mean if not that it is his dharmic responsibility to put the brakes on, as much as possible, to arrest this falling away in time which leads inexorably to a *pralaya*, or dissolution? The king cannot partially restore the *kṛta-yuga* except through exercising his power, his *daṇḍa*. The *daṇḍa*, literally the stick, symbolises his ability and duty to meter out punishment, to counteract as much as possible the evil tendencies of humanity in the *kali-yuga*. The function of the king consists then of steering, to his utmost, against the current of the stream pulling humanity along with it, and which finds its most explicit expression in the concept of *saṃsāra*, that defines the world as an incessant flow. As the representative of Varuṇa, the temporal ruler incarnates with his *daṇḍa* the aspect of 'rigour' (cf. above p. 48, n. 5) in the original pact made with the gods. As for the Brahmins, they take on the role of Mitra in this pact, and do their best to put all their efforts into repeating, through the sacrifice of which they are the masters, 'what the gods did in the beginning.' Now, the application of the *daṇḍa* represents the tamasic dimension of royal activity, as the *Sāṃkhya-kārikā* (12)[3] explains, which shows, incidentally, that the

3 The *Sāṃkhya-kārikā* (12) describe the activities of a king within

way of devotion preached in the *Bhagavad-gītā* has to be accompanied, in the dark age, by the way of fear and abstention from evil.

The responsibility for repressive social action in this ideal of a sacred royalty cannot be envisaged without the moral qualifications necessary to ensure the king is free from all vanity and personal interest. This is why the *Mahābhārata* explains, through the voice of Gāndhārī, the wife of Dhṛtarāṣṭra, that the first duty of a king is self-control and, above all, not to give in to desire or anger. She concludes: 'By defeating these two enemies [desire and anger] a king conquers the earth.... He who at first masters only himself, as if he were a country, does not seek to master his councilors and enemies in vain' (5, 127, 21 and 28).[4] Moreover, in the part which immediately follows the passage above, where Yudhiṣṭhira receives Bhīṣma's last instructions, the dynasty's elder statesman enumerates the thirty-six essential virtues and the thirty-six secondary ones necessary in the exercise of royal power. The king must be free of bitterness, attachment to worldly goods, and spite; he must be generous without being prodigal; he must protect his subjects, safeguard their prosperity and respect the Brahmins, etc. In the middle of enumerating all this, Bhīṣma also mentions

---

the framework of the three *guṇa* or qualities which compose the world: *sattva*, the good, luminous, ascendant quality; *rajas*, the expansive, passionate, horizontal quality; and *tamas*, the obscure, inert, descending quality. The role of the king is essentially rajasic through his exercise of power. But there is a sattvic consequence to this in the protection of the good and a tamasic element in the punishment of the wicked.

[4] Cited by Angelika Malinar (2012: 52).

that the king must never use the *daṇḍa* without having first fully examined the case of the person accused of a crime: *nāparīkṣya nayeddaṇḍam* (12, 70, 7). Now, it is interesting to note that the verb used in this context, *pari_ĪKṢ*, lends new meaning to the name Parīkṣit, Arjuna's grandson and the direct heir to Yudhiṣṭhira, who is thus 'He who examines,' like the vigilant king he is destined to become.[5]

Up until now we have spoken of Yudhiṣṭhira only indirectly. Now it is he, as the *dharmarājan*, who, as such, is called upon to fulfil the function of the ideal king in the world of the Bhārata. We must therefore pause for a while on this figure. Hiltebeitel thinks that Western commentators, with their reflex action of seeing a natural connection between the *Mahābhārata* and the *Iliad*, have underestimated the importance of this character. 'A lack of comparability' with regard to Achilles, with whom it is natural to compare him, has done him a disservice. However, for the Chicago Indologist he is the main hero of the *Mahābhārata*, which, as we have said, he considers to be 'A Reader's Guide to the Education of the Dharma King.' He says: 'I will argue that he is the real hero and also the "real king". Arjuna is ultimately a diversion' (2001: 46–47).[6]

---

5 In fact, this king's name can be written in two ways: Parīkṣit or Parikṣit. In the second case the name means 'He who surrounds' or 'He who stays around.'

6 If Dumézil also rejects the primacy of Arjuna, he dismisses as 'impossible interpretations' 'those who claim to detect in the poem a principal hero' ([1968] 1986: 1, 240). In *The Queen and the Avatar* (ch. 1) we put forward the idea that, contrary to what happens in some other epics, several characters take on

The latter, although he is believed by many to be the main hero, he continues in summary, forgets the most important teachings, and almost completely disappears at the end of the sixteenth book, whereas Vyāsa, as the supreme guide of his 'creatures', keeps a soft spot for Yudhiṣṭhira who 'never forgets anything.' Hiltebeitel's point of view seems to be related to the idea that an epic is only ever written in order to support imperialism as such, or at least some form of political regime. The composers of the *Mahābhārata* were thus, in his opinion, at the service of an imperialistic ideology, aimed at a dynasty reigning in the North of India at the time of the Maurya (322–184 BC) for whom Yudhiṣṭhira exemplifies the ideal type, due to his strongly brahmanic character.[7] This calls to mind the *Aeneid* where, through its Trojan mythology, Virgil confers an almost divine legitimacy on the emperor

---

the role of hero in turn in the *Mahābhārata*, according to the point of view adopted. Also to be noted is that, although he compares Achilles to Yudhiṣṭhira, Hiltebeitel uses elsewhere Dumézil's formula: Heracles-Vāyu-Bhīma and Achilles-Indra-Arjuna (1990: 220). From another point of view, Achilles' short temper brings him closer to Bhīma.

[7] Hiltebeitel does not seem to reject the hypothesis made by some scholars that the historical 'epic' of Alexander the Great, who travelled as far as India, played a role in the composition of the *Mahābhārata*. In fact, the Indian epic mentions more than once the Yavana (Ionians, Greeks), whose civilisation had a great influence on Indian culture from the time of the great Macedonian's journey. He also points out the model of the Huns mentioned at least six times in the *Mahābhārata* (*ibid.*, 30). But the latter arrived much later than Alexander in India (5th century AD), which creates problems of dating and assumes interpolations.

Augustus, or again, the *Iliad*, which according to André Sauge was written on the orders of Solon (2000).

In the same way that Kṛṣṇa-Vāsudeva has a special relationship with his cousin Arjuna, Kṛṣṇa-Dvaipāyana, alias Vyāsa, the other incarnation of Nārāyaṇa, has a close bond with Yudhiṣṭhira, of whom he is, genealogically speaking, the grandfather. This is why Hiltebeitel pays great attention to the parts where the old hermit talks directly to his grandson. Vyāsa appears at the death of Bhīṣma, as he lies on his bed of arrows, firstly to console Yudhiṣṭhira, who is present there too, and then to remind him of his duty. In fact, the *dharmarājan*, distraught by the massacre of the two armies and the loss of so many relatives, is on the point of giving up everything in order to follow the life of an ascetic. Moreover, it is really quite surprising that this hero, destined as he is to become king, never shows, either before or after his coronation, the slightest desire for power. Like his brother Arjuna, whom the *Bhagavad-gītā* describes as deeply reluctant to fight at the beginning of the battle against the Kaurava, Yudhiṣṭhira is forced to renounce his personal inclinations in order to follow his destiny as a *kṣatriya*. With the consent of Kṛṣṇa, who is also present at this scene, Vyāsa is obliged to put Yudhiṣṭhira firmly back on track: 'The earth is won by *kṣātradharma* (military duty). Enjoy it, son of Kuntī. Do not resist me' (Hiltebeitel, *ibid.*, 67). He then asks him to prepare for the *aśvamedha*, the horse sacrifice, which will inaugurate his new reign. Then he explains the procedure to him and gives him the names of all the people who will take part in it. It is to Arjuna that Yudhiṣṭhira has to entrust the particular task of following the horse in its meanderings, which will last an entire year. Let us recall here that before being sacrificed, the horse is set free to roam at ease wherever it wills for a year; all the territories that it crosses automatically becoming the property of the king.

Now, as to Yudhiṣṭhira's divine ancestry, it will be remembered that there is a difficulty here, in that this hero is the only one whose divine 'model', Dharma, is not a Vedic god. Dumézil seems to have resolved the problem by identifying Dharma with Mitra, in conformity with his thesis of the three functions. But Hiltebeitel does not agree with him on this point. He says: 'There is little to recommend Dumézil's view of Dharma as a "rejuvenated" Vedic Mitra' (*ibid.*, 138). Referring to several episodes in the story frame of the epic where Yama, the god of Death, is at one point ordained (*dīkṣita*, initiated) to complete an important sacrifice (*sattra*), the American scholar equates this other figure from the Vedic pantheon with Dharma, and thus with Yudhiṣṭhira. In initiating the battle of Kurukṣetra, Yudhiṣṭhira follows in the footsteps of the god of Death, who had elsewhere completed a *sattra* of sixty-one days where human victims replaced the usual animals. And in one case as in the other the goal is the same: to purge the earth of its population and then renew it. In support of this thesis, Hiltebeitel notably cites Bhaṭṭa Nārāyaṇa (eighth–ninth century), the author of a play who dramatises the scene where Bhīma gets his revenge on Duḥśāsana, who had dragged Draupadī by the hair after the dice game. Speaking to Draupadī, Bhīma says, 'In the sacrifice of war…, [the younger Pāṇḍavas] are the officiating priests; Lord Hari is the director of rites; the king [Yudhiṣṭhira] is the one consecrated (*dīkṣitaḥ*) for this sacrifice of war,

[our] wife is the one whose vow is maintained' (*ibid.*, 137).[8]

In fact, Hiltebeitel is not the only one to equate Dharma with Yama, and in the pages we have just cited he refers to five authors who have explored the question in this way. It is curious, however, that he does not recall in this context that in the *Mahābhārata*, Yama is often described as *dharmarājan*, like Yudhiṣṭhira. For his part, Alain Daniélou says: 'Yama is the god of death, the sovereign of the infernal regions. Sinister and fearful, he judges the dead whom his messengers drag before his throne. He is the embodiment of righteousness (*dharma*) and the king-of-justice (*dharma-rāja*). He is, however, amenable to pity' (1991: 132). And a few lines on he refers to the fact that he is also the master of the royal *daṇḍa*: 'Yama is punishment (*daṇḍa*), the Eternal Law on which the universe rests, for "the whole world rests on the law"' (*Mahābhārata*, 12, 4407). So it can be seen that there is more than one feature in common between Yama and Yudhiṣṭhira's functions, without counting their ontological relationship with the destructiveness of time.

Having said that, there do exist important differences between the two figures, because, after all, Yama, as Daniélou describes him, is sinister and fearful, ugly and deformed, traits which the Pāṇḍava king does not seem to have inherited at all. But it is not mandatory to take after one's father in every way. And perhaps in this disparity lies one of the astonishing 'psychological'

8 Draupadī vowed never to wash her hair until she had been revenged and could wash it in Duḥśāsana's blood.

twists, so often found in 'fiction', which are scattered throughout the epic and lend it such piquancy: could not this problematic ancestry of his be the cause of the evident lack of spirit that this king shows, in spite of himself, in the exercise of his power?

Another character trait of Yudhiṣṭhira's that Hiltebeitel observes is his association with dogs. He notes that: 'Yudhiṣṭhira, a portion of Yama-Dharma consecrated to carry out the battle of Kurukṣetra ... punctuates his career by a series of meditations on dogs.' For example, horrified by the devastation caused by the war which he has actually won, Yudhiṣṭhira says: 'We are not dogs, but we are like dogs greedy for a piece of meat. And now our meat has disappeared, and those who would eat the meat have vanished too' (2001: 171). The particular relationship that Yudhiṣṭhira has with dogs culminates in the final episode of his terrestrial existence. A mysterious dog accompanies him on his pilgrimage towards the Himalaya, from whence he will be taken up to Heaven. On the way Yudhiṣṭhira has lost his wife and his four brothers. He is now welcomed by Indra, who invites him to ascend to him on condition that he abandons his faithful companion, but three times the king stands by his vow not to betray a *bhakta*, a devotee, even if this be at the price of his ascension to the abode of Indra. It is then that the dog takes on his true form and reveals his identity as a manifestation of the god Dharma, the father of Yudhiṣṭhira. Satisfied by the way his son has dealt with this final initiatic ordeal, Dharma allows him into Heaven where he is the only one of the five brothers and their wife who enters while still in the body.

Hiltebeitel, however, does not give the traditional key to the relationship between Yudhiṣṭhira and dogs. In some images of Viṣṇu and in certain temples consecrated to him, such as in Puri in Orissa, there can be seen four animals, representing the four castes. The lion is associated with the Brahmins, the horse with the *kṣatriya*, the ox with the *vaiśya* and the dog with the *śūdra*. This association of the lion with Brahmins may be surprising to some, but the link between the king of the animals and the sacerdotal caste is altogether universal, even if it is more often used as an emblem of royalty. The association of the horse and the ox with the warrior and the peasant is, in contrast, perfectly clear, as is the association of dogs with the servant whose specific quality is fidelity. If we take into account the fact that the *Mahābhārata* is clearly addressed to all the men of the fourth age in whom, as we have seen above (ch. 3), the mentality of the fourth caste, the *śūdra*, predominates, it makes complete sense that the god Dharma, on the threshold of the *kali-yuga*, would take on the modest appearance of a dog in the key episode where he reveals himself to his son. Finally, the essential link connecting Dharma with the fourth caste not only appears in the episode where he assumes the guise of a dog, but is also evident in the fact that not only does he incarnate as Yudhiṣṭhira, but also as the third son of Vyāsa, Vidura. The mother of this latter is in fact an obscure servant, a *śūdra*, whom Ambikā has surreptitiously slipped into the bed of the repulsive hermit to take her place, in order to avoid sleeping with him a second time.[9]

9 Dharma is forced to be reborn in this way because of the curse of the *ṛṣi* Māṇḍavya, whom he had punished in an

In addition, this canine avatar of Dharma's reinforces Yudhiṣṭhira's possible association with Yama, the god of death, and no doubt it is not by chance that he manifests himself in such a guise to his son at the moment when Yudhiṣṭhira is on the point of leaving the world. For it is a common feature of a number of mythologies that the dog, from Anubis to Cerberus, is portrayed as a psychopomp animal, closely associated with death and the afterlife. India is no exception to this, for 'Yama owns two four-eyed dogs with wide nostrils, who were born to the Fleet-One (Saramā), the bitch who guards the herds of Indra. They watch the path of the dead' (Daniélou 1991: 134).

These considerations should allow us, hopefully, to shed new light on the mysterious figure of Śaunaka, the Son of a Dog. We have already seen that this master of the ritual sacrifice, to whom the history of the war is recounted in the story frame of the epic (cf. ch. 3), could well be, according to Hiltebeitel, none other than the 'true' author of the *Mahābhārata*. Even if, to our knowledge, he is nowhere represented as an incarnation of Dharma, he is, however, the first to pay a visit to Yudhiṣṭhira in the forest where the eldest Pāṇḍava is exiled, and it is he who, before all the other sages that we will mention further on (ch. 12), defines for this special

excessive manner for a small fault: the *ṛṣi* was impaled for having impaled an insect in his childhood! This strange story shows how the law of retaliation can no longer be applied in the last age (cf. Hiltebeitel, 2001:192–5). As for the dharmic relationship between Vidura and Yudhiṣṭhira, it is highlighted by an amazing miracle: when Vidura dies, his soul passes into the soul of Yudhiṣṭhira.

disciple the tasks of the dharmic king, thus assuring the transmission of the Vedic heritage down through the generations to the end of the cycle.

12

Trickery in the *Mahābhārata*, a Sign of the Age of Kali

On many occasions, and above all during the decisive battle between the clans, Kṛṣṇa, the avatar, the supreme divinity incarnate, exhorts his companions to use stratagems that their code of honour, especially as found in the *kṣatriya* code of conduct, condemns outright. Much ink has flowed over this problematic behaviour and it has discomfited both Orientalists and Hindus alike. Here, for the record, are some of the most well-known of these transgressions. Seeing the Pāṇḍava incapable of defeating Droṇa, the commander of the enemy army, Kṛṣṇa counsels them to kill an elephant by the name of Aśvatthāman—the same name as the son of their opponent. Even Yudhiṣṭhira, the incarnation of righteousness, of *dharma*, was finally convinced to lie to his old guru—it was admittedly only by omission—and he kept quiet about the true identity of the Aśvatthāman killed in this deception. This is how Droṇa, who is completely thrown by all of this, allows himself to be vanquished without putting up the slightest resistance to Dhṛṣtadyumna. Later, in the final battle that pits him against Karṇa, Arjuna is told by the avatar to shoot a fatal arrow at his half-brother, who, totally unarmed, is struggling to heave the wheel of his chariot out of a rut in the battlefield. Finally, when Bhīma, wielding his mace, confronts the terrible Duryodhana during their final battle, Kṛṣṇa again, seeing him in great danger, tells him to strike his assailant on the thigh, contrary to all the rules of chivalry which forbid any hitting below the belt. This enumeration of apparently criminal faults does not stop there, but it should not be necessary to amplify any further to get a clear idea of the nature of the problem.

During the course of their military and ethical training, the five Pāṇḍava receive, from the time of their education at the court of Dhṛtarāṣṭra onwards, the teachings of numerous sages, starting with Droṇa, their master-at-arms, Bhīṣma, their great-uncle, and later on their cousin Kṛṣṇa, whom they consult on more than one occasion. Because of the royal position Yudhiṣṭhira is destined to assume, he is the most concerned in this ethical apprenticeship, and during his exile in the forest the Vedic priest Śaunaka (cf. ch. 11), the chaplain Dhaumya, the *ṛṣi* Nārada and Mārkaṇḍeya, and the sage Bṛhadaśva all deliver long speeches to him on this subject. We have also seen that Vyāsa himself keeps in close contact with him. The virtues advocated by these eminent gurus can, for the most part, be found in the *Upaniṣad*. But they are the subject of greater attention in the epic. The insistence on setting standards of behaviour is most likely an important consequence of the Brahmanic reaction to the spread of Buddhist ideas. The exalted virtues are thus strongly linked to the specific characteristics of the castes and are largely codifiable, from Dumézil's point of view, by the tripartite function.

But if the list of the heroes' virtues is quite unsurprising and conventional, what can be said about their vices and lapses in conduct? And how, above all, can one understand that Kṛṣṇa, the supreme divinity come down to earth to reestablish *dharma*, allows himself, once war has been declared, to permit and even encourage adharmic and irregular behaviour, in flagrant contradiction to the moral precepts so often repeated? The ravings of the Indologist Hopkins and his *Inversion Theory*, who once believed, along with a string of followers, that in the transgressions committed by the Pāṇḍava could be found proof that the *Mahābhārata* was originally written to the glory of the Kaurava, and that it had been changed (rather awkwardly!) later on in support of the opposite clan, can be safely ignored. No one anymore, at least not to our knowledge, espouses such a theory. It is to Dumézil that we must turn to find the first intelligent approach to the subject. Through him we find out that the apparently reprehensible behaviour of heroes is a constant theme in Indo-European mythology, a factor which he documents copiously.[1] But here we will only concentrate on the case of the *Mahābhārata*. In the epic it is above all Yudhiṣṭhira who is involved, as it is he who will repeat in epic mode, what Dumézil calls the 'sins of sovereignty'. He 'repeats' them because these sins have an earlier model. They recall, in one way or

---

[1] Besides *Myth and Epic* already cited on this subject, see also *The Destiny of the Warrior* (1970) where this theme is also examined in a number of Indo-European myths.

another, those of Indra as related in the *Brāhmaṇa*. The king of the Vedic gods is far from having an irreproachable character. He has killed a Brahmin, the ultimate crime in the Indian consciousness, gone back on his word and seduced the wife of a *ṛṣi*. These three transgressions make him lose, momentarily, his lustre (*tejas*), strength (*bala*) and his beauty (*rūpa*), and force him to seek redemption. We can recognise in this triad the trifunctional structure. It will take us too far away from our topic if we plunge here into the mass of data showing all the subtle correlations between the Vedic god and the epic hero, a subject treated in minuscule detail by Hiltebeitel (1990: ch. 9). So we will limit ourselves to a few essential points taken from his analyses. It will be recalled that the five Pāṇḍava are also regarded as the manifestation of a quintuple Indra. But although it is Arjuna, as the specific incarnation of the latter, who possesses most of his qualities, it is his older brother who carries the burden of assuming his principal 'errors'. Yudhiṣṭhira will later reproach himself for his faults after the war. He lists them in a kind of *mea culpa*, berating himself for his attitude in the fighting which led to the deaths of the great opposing generals, Bhīṣma, Droṇa and Karṇa, and finally blaming himself for the death of Abhimanyu (*ibid.*: 239–240). This remorse explains, at least in part, his desire to renounce power in favour of the ascetic life of purification. It takes all of Kṛṣṇa's powers of persuasion to deter him from this plan, and the avatar plays a similar role here, *mutatis mutandis*, to Viṣṇu's role with Indra in the *Ṛg-veda* (cf. 1, 22, 19). Viṣṇu, still subordinate to Indra, is portrayed here as his close friend (*yujyaḥ śakha*), preparing conquests for him by opening up space with his three strides (cf. ch. 6).

For Hiltebeitel, each Kaurava general incarnates a transgression against *dharma* which can only be rectified by actions imbued with the symbolic corresponding fault. He even sees in the successive Pāṇḍava victories over the four great enemy chiefs a sort of 'ladder of descent to the earth' (*ibid.*, 284), which echoes in a condensed fashion the series of the four *yuga*, and the four socio-religious castes, the *varṇa*, which characterise them. Finally, he finds in this new context the symbolism of the colours seen above (ch. 3). Bhīṣma is thus associated with white (he has white weapons, clothes, and horses), Droṇa with red (he has red horses), Karṇa with yellow, the colour of the sun, and Śalya with black, the colour of the earth (*ibid.*, 283).

The war as a quest for supremacy over the three worlds has a ritual dimension that taints the sacrificer(s) with a form of uncleanliness or impurity. 'According to *Śatapatha Brāhmaṇa* 12, 8, 2, 32, "one might secure these three worlds by three victims".' But, '... the taking of animal victims (*paśu*) involves impurities and dangers which must be neutralised. It is not different in the epic' (*ibid.*, 287). In epic mode the filth involved in the bloody sacrifice becomes transformed into a moral defilement, and the need for this corruption is thus summarised by Kṛṣṇa himself: 'Enemies of superior number are to be slain falsely [*mithyāvadhās*], as also by stratagems [*upāyair*]. This path [*mārga*] was formerly followed when the gods were slayers of the Asuras. A path followed by the good [*sadbhis*] may be trodden by all' (9, 60, 62; *ibid.*, 290). And he goes so far as to say to Yudhiṣṭhira that lies (*anṛta*), at least in certain situations, can be better than the truth: *satyājjyāyo 'nṛtaṃ bhavet* (*ibid.*, 251).

If the behaviour of the avatar sometimes surprises or even shocks, it should not be forgotten that this licence, granted only in certain situations, is subject to a rigorous condition. Kṛṣṇa emphasises in the *Bhagavad-gītā* the fact that the way of the warrior implies perfect detachment regarding the fruits of action, and the complete renunciation of personal gain. Such an attitude has two main consequences. First of all, it leads to a sort of redemption for the victim, provided he has fought according to his duty as a *kṣatriya*, which is what explains the immediate ascension of Duryodhana to Heaven, welcomed with a rain of flowers at the moment of his death. Then, having in a certain manner taken on the filth of the opponent, the winners are obliged to make atonement. This is why Vyāsa, in the twelfth book (34ff.), teaches that *dharma* can sometimes take the form of *adharma*, explaining to Yudhiṣṭhira that since he was forced to follow this particular divine way against his will because of the fault of another, and that he repented it afterwards, he must now accomplish the great horse sacrifice (*aśvamedha*) to purify himself and ensure the prosperity of the kingdom.

In *The Queen and the Avatar* (pp. 71–74) we discussed this subject by comparing Kṛṣṇa's attitude to lying and using tricks like Jacob's and Ulysses', in cyclical circumstances similar to those described in the *Mahābhārata*.[2] We will return to this briefly in an attempt to resolve the

---

2 This means that, along with the Guenonian Gaston Georgel (1976: 202), we would place the biblical patriarchs from Abraham to Jacob at a point in the cycle of humanity comparable to the first half of the iron age of the Greeks and the Hindus.

moral difficulty posed by these transgressions of Kṛṣṇa's, but with a slightly different focus than before. This is what Schuon says about the biblical prophet:

> The unadvised reader finds it strange, to say the least, that Jacob, at the instigation of Rebecca but also of his own will, deceives Isaac, his father, by posing as Esau; in reality there was no immoral initiative but a conflict of planes; a particular divine will ran counter to a social situation. For even though Esau was the eldest he was visibly unworthy of his birthright, which he sold unbeknownst to his father; if there was deceit, it was above all here. In saying 'I am Esau,' Jacob meant, 'I am what Esau ought to be, but could not and would not be'; hence 'I am the true Esau.' If there is a fault it is also on the part of Isaac, who had an all but blind preference for his elder son despite the disqualification of the latter; in the end, Isaac recognised Jacob's priority, Jacob and Esau were reconciled, and God sanctioned the situation, which proves that Jacob and his mother were right (1982: 129).

Let us note, as a preliminary remark, that the biblical story contains, despite important differences, two astonishing analogies with the Indian epic: on the one hand, Isaac, like Dhṛtarāṣṭra, is blind, at least at the end of his life, and on the other hand, the overall goal is the same, to justify the transfer of authority not to the eldest in the family, but to a younger member who is better qualified. Now, this is very much the situation with the Pāṇḍava, who are the younger branch of the lunar dynasty in relation to the Kaurava.

There is also perhaps, in Kṛṣṇa's maneuvers to overthrow this hierarchical order of birth, a remembrance or a repetition of what happened at the beginning of creation, in 'the eternal beginning' when the *asura*, created before the *deva*,[3] were supplanted by them. One can even find there an echo of the original myth which Coomaraswamy makes explicit when he says:

> In this eternal beginning there is only the Supreme Identity of 'That One' (*tad ekam*), without differentiation of being from non-being, light from darkness, or separation of sky from earth. The All is for the present impounded in the first principle, which may be spoken of as the Person, Progenitor, Mountain, Tree, Dragon or endless Serpent. Related to this principle by filiation or *younger brotherhood* [our italics] and *alter ego* rather than another principle, is the Dragon-slayer, born to supplant the Father and take possession of the kingdom, distributing its treasures to his followers (1999: 6).

In all cases this mythical motif of the usurpation of power by an older brother and its retrieval by a younger brother is a constant aspect of the divine play correcting the centrifugal nature of creation through reparation based on a sacrifice.

---

3 'There are two kinds of descendants of Prājāpati, the *deva* and the *asura*. Now the *deva* were indeed the younger, the *asura* the elder ones' (*Bṛhadāraṇyakopaniṣad*, 1, 3, 1).

By definition, and this definition comes from the *Bhagavad-gītā* itself, Kṛṣṇa is the supreme Principle necessarily situated beyond good and evil, or, as in the Hindu perspective, beyond *dharma* and *adharma*. This means that he cannot be judged by a morality that concerns only man. In that he incarnates Viṣṇu he is called upon, in his task of preserving the world, to take the side of the camp where *dharma* predominates, and this is what matters. *Adharmika* behaviour (contrary to *dharma*), within the context of his earthly life is thus justified to the extent that, on a higher level, of which men may not necessarily be aware, he restores or affirms the essential *dharma*. The logic is the same as in the case of Jacob: if there is deception, it is in Śakuni and Duryodhana's loaded dice. The principle of compensation for the heroes' sins, unhampered by Dumézil and Hiltebeitel, retains here all its relevance. What Kṛṣṇa's enigmatic behaviour involves in the last analysis is the play of *māyā*, the power of divine illusion. As the avatar says: 'The Lord (*īśvara*) dwells in the hearts of all beings, O Arjuna, and by his power of illusion he sets in motion all beings, which are mounted on a machine' (*Bhagavad-gītā*, 18, 61). The word translated here as machine (*yantra*) is polysemous, since it designates not only any instrument or tool without awareness, but also a sacred diagram having magic powers.[4] In this context it refers, *a priori*, to the chariot of the warrior, meaning the vital support of the individual soul. Accepting this abstruse dimension of the divinity, who does as It wills, according to a Qur'anic expression—even if It were

[4] Etymologically a *yantra* is a support or a link which holds something in place.

incarnated in the person of a 'tricky mortal' (Hopkins)—depends ultimately on the same act of faith which obliges us to admit that God permits evil for our highest good. Rāmakṛṣṇa comments on this mystery: 'Poison within the teeth of a snake causes no harm to it. But that poison injected into others causes death to them. Similarly *Maya* that is in Iswara causes Him no harm. Rather, it is an adorable attribute of His. And this *Maya* keeps all beings in bondage' (quoted by Chidbhavananda, 1969: 947).

Now, divine *māyā* is an aspect of the infinitude of God, who cannot not create the world at the risk of limiting the full potentiality intrinsic to Him. But the world is not God and so cannot be perfect, from whence stem all evils and inevitable shadows. In Vedantine terms, manifestation is only an illusion, and what saves man is that his individual soul is nothing other, in the last analysis, than the Absolute, the *brahman*: *brahma satyaṃ jaganmithyā jīvo brahmaiva nāparaḥ*, 'the *brahman* is true, the world is illusory, the individual soul is nothing other than the *brahman*' (Śaṅkara, *Brahmajñānāvalīmālā*, 20). Certainly we find it extremely difficult to consider all suffering or injustice as being illusory, but such is the weight of the outward ego, and the spiritual man sees in the trials of this lower world a way of return to the essential. Now, the world not being God is subject to time, to becoming and impermanence, which means that it has a life and a death, and that this 'death' is followed by a new creation, *ad infinitum*. Such at least is the Hindu doctrine which is also found elsewhere, as for example with the Stoics, who conceived the life of the world in an altogether similar way. Now, since the world is at the end of the cycle, it is becoming increasingly opaque, as we have seen in the theory of the four ages, and this merely negative evolution justifies in the eyes of Hindus the need to resort to means which, like the tricks and lies authorised by Kṛṣṇa, allow for the safeguarding of *dharma* for as long as possible.

A last point remains to be examined with regard to the sins of the heroes. The law of *karman* means that all action has a consequence on its own plane. Thus, despite his ruse being in accord with the divine plan, Jacob has to pay for his culpable behaviour within the contingent framework of his earthly life: 'in the opinion of the rabbis, Jacob nevertheless had to expiate the appearance of fraud by all that he had to suffer later on, above all from his own sons' (Schuon: *ibid.*, 130). And David would also shed bitter tears over the loss of his first son born from the adulterous liaison with Bathsheba before seeing this union vindicated in the birth of Solomon (II Samuel, 3). Neither do the Pāṇḍava escape this inexorable law. They witness their five respective sons, born to Draupadī, massacred after the war by the bloodthirsty Aśvatthāman, and we have seen how Yudhiṣṭhira has to be purified of his lie by accomplishing the horse sacrifice (*aśvamedha*). It is also because of their transgressions against *dharma* that they have to spend a brief sojourn in hell before being glorified. As for Kṛṣṇa himself, he can do nothing to stop Gāndhārī cursing all the people of the Vṛṣṇi, of whom he is king, to annihilation.

13

The *Mahābhārata* is in the Soul

IN THE CHRISTIAN WORLD, the Church Fathers greatly emphasise the fact that the Scriptures contain multiple levels of meaning that are in some way juxtaposed. They have found in this juxtaposition an inexhaustible source of inspiration for their historical, mystical, symbolical and theological commentaries, which they have not ceased to imbibe from over the course of many centuries. They have described these levels of meaning in numerous ways, and beyond the consideration that it is useless to wish to artificially limit a theoretically indefinite number of possibilities, they have generally reduced their speculations to three, four or seven levels of meaning. A sort of 'theology of the four meanings', in Father de Lubac's words, has finally prevailed, with nevertheless several terminological variations and different orderings.[1] To be brief we will only cite here the list Dante uses

1 On this question we have mainly consulted Father Henri de Lubac's essay: *Medieval Exegesis, The Four Senses of Scripture* (2000). This book, which contains a veritable treasure-trove of traditional, symbolical interpretations, is fundamental, even though its exhaustive ambitions, its rather confusing presenta-

in the *Convivio* (2, 1), which takes account of the literal, allegorical, moral and anagogic meanings, and which is probably the most common. If we refer to the Florentine poet's scheme more than to that of a particular Father or Doctor of the Church, it is because it has the advantage of opening this interpretative method to domains other than Scripture in the strictest sense of the word. It can be applied to literature, as Dante himself did, as well as to all the arts, *mutatis mutandis*. In the field of architecture, for instance, a cathedral is thus a place of worship on the literal plane, but allegorically it represents the Church as the community of Christians, then morally,[2] by its cruciform layout, the Passion of Christ, and anagogically the inner man in his deiform dimension.

Like all myth, legend or epic, the *Mahābhārata* easily lends itself to interpretations of this kind. Particularly to an anagogic commentary, that is to say, a commentary that 'opens onto the higher', consisting in bringing all the events in stories back to the inward drama of the human soul. Such an exegesis, here as elsewhere, is a sort of touchstone for the truth and efficacy of traditional stories. Speaking of the *Rāmāyaṇa*, Schuon says, for example:

> The doctrine of *Rama* is contained in the *Ramayana*: the myth retraces the destiny of the soul (*Sita*)

---

tion and its profusion of long untranslated Latin quotations make it rather difficult to use. We long to read a more condensed and widely accessible version.

2 We have seen that there are significant variations in the use of words designating the four meanings, and the moral plane is often qualified as tropological. Whatever the case may be, it is not here a question of morality in the usual sense of the term.

> ravished by passion and ignorance (*Ravana*) and exiled in matter at the confines of the cosmos (*Lanka*). Every soul given up to *Shri Rama* is identified with *Sita*, the heroine carried off and then delivered.

To which he adds in a note:

> the testing of *Sita—Rama* doubting her fidelity—refers to the discontinuity between the 'I' and the 'Self', to the hiatus in the incommensurable dialogue between the soul and the Lord; the repudiation of *Sita* and her return to her mother the Earth signifies that the ego as such remains always the ego. But the eternal *Sita* is none other than *Lakshmi*, spouse of *Rama-Vishnu*, and she it is who, *in divinis*, is the prototype of the soul (1961: 144).

Regarding the *Mahābhārata*, any anagogic approach must necessarily take as its starting point what Kṛṣṇa says in the *Bhagavad-gītā*: 'I am the Self (*ātman*), O Guḍākeśa [Arjuna], seated in the heart of all beings' (10, 20). What is more, the two Kṛṣṇa (*kṛṣṇau*: cf. ch. 3), Nara and Nārāyaṇa, represent the self and the Self, that is the two birds mentioned in the *Upaniṣad* (cf. ch. 9), present in each man, and the battlefield, Kurukṣetra, the field of Kuru, is none other than the body: 'O son of Kuntī, this body is called the field (*kṣetra*). He who knows this is called by the sages the knower of the field (*kṣetra-jña*)' (*ibid.*, 13, 1). We have also seen above (ch. 9) the application of this statement to the symbolism of the chariot. From this it can be seen that all the protagonists of the great battle, of the epic psychomachy,[3] necessarily incarnate the different faculties of the soul struggling against itself within its earthly destiny. Hindu commentators, scholars, sages and spiritual masters continually have recourse to interpretations derived from this way of seeing things, and one can find examples of these scattered throughout traditional literature. The oldest attempt at a systematic anagogic approach to the epics is probably Madhva's, the founder of the dualist school, *Dvaitavāda* or *Dvaitavedānta* (thirteenth century). In his *Mahābhārata-tātparya-nirṇaya* (*Enquiry into the Mahābhārata*) he starts from the principle that the *Bhārata*, just like the *Rāmāyaṇa* which he also discusses at length, is in the soul, in the individual, in the microcosm (*adhyātmani stha*), which is difficult to imagine, he says, even for the gods (*sura*)!

In modern times, the Hindu scholar V. S. Sukthankar ([1942], 1957), inspired by this classical attempt, developed in part a similar interpretation on three of the levels of reading expounded in the Christian tradition—which he seems incidentally not to have known of—that is to say, the literal, moral and anagogic, which he calls the mundane, ethical and metaphysical planes.[4]

---

3 Psychomachy is the struggle all men experience in their soul. It is also the title (*Psychomachia*) of a very famous poem of the middle ages by the Latin Christian writer Prudentius (end 4th, beginning 5th century) who portrays, with an epic verve inspired by Virgil, the fight between personified Virtues and Vices.

4 If we had to add to this tripartition an allegorical key, we would immediately consider everything that had been said about the epic's heroes in relation to the gods they embody.

The ethical dimension of the epic is, for him, above all found in the passages where *dharma* is defined, in the countless rules of conduct that refer to or rely on it. Its natural framework is the opposition between *dharma* and *adharma*, or the antagonism between the *deva* and the *asura*. On the level which he calls metaphysical, Sukthankar suggests the following correspondences: Dhṛtarāṣṭra, 'He who has a firm kingdom' or, better still in the context, 'He who has seized the kingdom,' is the ego whose blindness is well known and which constantly refers everything back to itself. His one hundred sons, with Duryodhana at their head—a character who, for our part, can be easily associated with pride—represent the negative or asuric tendencies of the soul, its vices, if one will. The wise Vidura, Dhṛtarāṣṭra's half-brother, who is always at his side, incarnates *buddhi*, the intelligence or the conscience. The blind king wants to consult him all the time and has no difficulty recognising the truth of what he says, but he never follows his point of view, pandering as he does at the critical moment to the badgering of his oldest son, who takes advantage of the obvious weakness of his character. Old Bhīṣma, who has renounced the kingdom and marriage, and who has the power to choose the moment of his death, represents memory whose authority seems to skip the vagaries of time, and whom the combatants on the two sides consult at critical moments.

On the opposing side, Sukthankar concentrates predominantly on the two occupants of the chariot, Kṛṣṇa, the inward man, and Arjuna, the outward man, who is totally devoted to his master in the decisive engagement of the inner battle, which is the greater holy war. His analysis tallies perfectly with what was said above on this symbolism (ch. 9). Unfortunately, in contrast, the Indian scholar says nothing about the Pāṇḍava brothers who, as certain Brahmins have explained to us, can be identified with the five senses, *indriya*, or faculties of Indra (cf. also ch. 9). Constantly listening out for teachings on *dharma*, as he does, Yudhiṣṭhira corresponds to hearing; Bhīma, the son of the wind, associated by birth with the air, personifies the sense of touch; Arjuna, the archer with an infallible eye, is sight; and the twins, Nakula and Sahadeva, connected to nourishing earth, are respectively taste and smell. The order of their birth is thus identical to the order given by the *Sāṃkhya* in its list of the senses and the elements associated with them, that is, ether, air, fire, water and earth. As for *manas*, the inner sense which Draupadī represents in this perspective, it is cited in the correct position at the end of this list. Jean Varenne says: 'The six senses of man are, in Brahmanical texts, constantly considered as divinities; they are in fact powers similar to cosmic forces. As such, they constitute one of the stakes in the rivalry between the Gods and the Asura' (1967: 182). And the *Bṛhadāraṇyakopaniṣad* (1, 3) shows, for example, how the *deva* fight against the *asura* by means of a Vedic chant (*udgītha*) during a sacrifice in order to win back the senses stolen by them. Although the fight in question is applied to a different list of senses, since it concerns the voice, the breath, sight, hearing and *manas*—in that order—it nevertheless sheds light on the battle between the Pāṇḍava and the Kaurava.

This type of interpretation, which is quite clear as to the generalities, has nevertheless a certain fluidity[5] which

5 Witness the equivalences provided (without source) by

can lead, if too systematically applied, to forced readings. Perhaps it is for this reason that it is practically never mentioned in Orientalist scholarly literature. At any rate, few seem to be interested in drawing spiritual lessons from the texts they examine. Yet this form of interpretation cannot be done away with, as its relevance is obvious. It is necessary to take into account the microcosmic or inward dimension of the universal combat, not only because of the teachings of the *Bhagavad-gītā* and other didactic passages from the epic, but also because of the nature of things and the universality of symbolism. As Martin Lings says, in a work already quoted (cf. ch. 8): 'Civil war is a most adequate symbol of the fallen soul, which is by definition at war with itself' (1996: 17). One wonders, moreover, how a narrative of such universal stature, whatever its degree of inspiration might be, could otherwise gain such a perennial and efficacious standing. The half-hearted opinion of Hiltebeitel, who quotes Sukhtankar in passing, is all the more curious:

> After all, such a psychology becomes intelligible in a religious tradition which places such regular emphasis on the belief that the divine is found in every man, the center to which all else relates.

Rivière (1979: 54–55). If this writer agrees *grosso modo* with Sukhtankar regarding Dhṛtarāṣṭra, Duryodhana and the Kaurava, and if he mentions the link between the Pāṇḍava and *tattva*, the principles of *Sāṃkhya*, he makes Bhīṣma into 'blind faith and the ancestral fear which religions inculcate'! Other more or less happy equivalences given by him are the following: he sees in Sañjaya intuition, in Drupada intuitive knowledge and in Subhadrā goodness.

> One would hardly expect a psychology like this from Homer (1990: 43).

The *Iliad* has however been the subject of more than one anagogic reading, and echoes of it can even be found in the alchemical tradition.[6] In pitting the Greek side, supported by Juno (marriage, duty), against the Trojans guided by Venus (love), Virgil portrayed a real psychomachy. In the drama of Aeneas, he inaugurated what is called in Shakespeare the conflict between passion and reason, and what the French refer to as *le dilemme cornélien*.

We cannot conclude this chapter without mentioning once more a text which we also referred to in *The Queen and the Avatar* (p. 112), the *Kṛṣṇopaniṣad*, which, although quite a late text, explodes like the finale at a fireworks display, rich in its infinitude of novel symbolic meanings:

> The personified Vedas and personified Upanisads became 16,108 women whose forms were perfectly spiritual. Personified hatred became the wrestler Canura. Personified envy became Mustika. Personified arrogance became Kuvalayapida. Personified pride became the demonic bird Baka. Personified mercy became Mother Rohini. The earth goddess became Satyabhama. Personified disease became Aghasura. Personified quarrel became King Kamsa. Personified peacefulness became the Lord's friend Sudama. Personified truthfulness became Akrura. Personified self-

---

6 For example, Dom Joseph Pernety in *Les Fables égyptiennes et grecques évoilées et réduites au même principe, avec une explication des hiéroglyphes et de la guerre de Troye* (see Bibliography).

control became Uddhava. Lord Visnu Himself became Krishna's conch shell, which made a roar like thunder and which, also born from the milk-ocean, was the goddess of fortune's kinsman. Breaking a pot to steal yogurt, Lord Krishna created an ocean of milk. In this way the Lord became a child and enjoyed pastimes as He had before in the great ocean (of milk). Lord Krishna appeared to remove His enemies and protect (His devotees) (*Kṛṣṇopaniṣad*, 1, 13–18).

This shower of correspondences shows the extent to which the tradition remains completely free in its use of symbols, beyond any systematic organisation. Included in this *Upaniṣad* can be found more than one theme discussed in the preceding pages: Rohinī embodies Mercy; Akrura, Truthfulness; Uddhava, Self-control, etc, as in the anagogic interpetations we have referred to. In breaking the butter jars to get at the contents, the child Kṛṣṇa evokes Viṣṇu, the All-penetrating, the master of all the latent possibilities of manifestation symbolised by the ocean of milk. His divine play upsets the peace of society: he has to 'pay' for this transgression on the human level, being tied by a rope to a heavy mortar by his adoptive mother, Yaśodā, who is forced to punish him.[7] His 16,108 lovers are the verses of the Scripture, and too bad for those who are shocked by such erotic extravagance! The symbol is a matter of transparency and one only needs eyes to see it. True tradition is not

7 In receiving on his bed the visit of Arjuna and Duryodhana, Kṛṣṇa evokes Nārāyaṇa sleeping and dreaming on the same ocean of milk.

and cannot be, on pain of drying up, anything other than a living reality, quick to renew itself in order to maintain men's faith and satisfy their appetite for beauty and wonder. Its survival through the centuries is at this price.

Conclusion

The first Western scholars of the *Mahābhārata*, obsessed with a short-sighted methodology, described the epic as a junkyard, a 'monstrous chaos' (*ungeheuerliches Chaos, sic* Oldenberg, a German Indologist at the beginning of the 20th century, cited by everyone for this peremptory opinion), a poorly conceived jumble of disparate legends created by different schools of diverse thought who could only have elaborated them over the course of several centuries. Fortunately, Indology has positively evolved since then, and has produced some eminent researchers who have started to perceive in the text something other than an amalgam of heterogeneous literary snippets, vague historical reminiscences and pseudo-philosophical quibbles created by a punctilious caste particularly anxious to protect its social ascendancy. Dumézil, Biardeau and Hiltebeitel, to cite only three authors who have particularly caught our attention and who represent the cream of recent research on this subject, provide a vision, or rather, deeper visions of the epic, constituting a series of undeniable achievements. By enriching their field of study with the help of modern sciences such as history, sociology, anthropology, comparative mythology, literary analysis and the study of religious phenomena, they have certainly brought some interesting insights to the Indian scene, with the merit of having in common the fact that they have all refrained from systematically considering any difficult passages, and notably any didactic digressions in the epic recital, as a later interpolation. The relevance of Orientalist efforts grows, in our opinion, to the extent that their analyses overcome the ethnocentric prejudices which so often mired the first Western attempts. One owes to recent research the clarification of many ritual reminiscences, synchronic or diachronic parallel myths and social paradigms generating so many constituent elements of Brahmanic ideology.

Certainly, in only citing from time to time the works of these scholars who have spent their entire lives exploring every inch of the *Mahābhārata*, we have not been able to render sufficient justice to their efforts. The careful reader wishing to learn more is therefore invited to find in their works many other paths of enquiry, demanding, fascinating, whatever the case may be. But to read these copious writings, and to learn, for example, that the *Mahābhārata* contains an encrypted doctrine of the trifunctional structure of Indo-European society (Dumézil), that it is a manifestation of the reaction of Brahmanic ideology to the expansion of Buddhism (Biardeau),[1] that it thus reaffirms the political and ideological supremacy of a particular caste in the social reality of India (Bronkhorst), that it is a guide to the education of the Dharma King (Hiltebeitel), or that it is the

[1] Let us however pay a fairer tribute to this Indologist whose work is not only limited to this thesis. Among her peers, Biardeau is the most 'Hindu', as described by Hiltebeitel.

allegorical fable of an astrological mutation (Lerner), makes it very hard to understand why millions of people over the course of time have seen in the epic a sacred text. One wonders how the faithful of all castes have found existential and spiritual reference points susceptible of guiding them on the inward journey of their lives, and this well beyond the *kṣatriya* milieu, which the epic seems to address *a priori*. The omnipresence of the *Mahābhārata* in Indian life is such that it led Jean-Claude Carrière, who produced, along with Peter Brook, a quasi-Shakespearean theatrical version of it, to wonder, not without some truth, if this work, along with the *Rāmāyaṇa*, 'did not constitute the invisible glue which makes so many people one people' (2001: 13). There is here a mystery which transcends all the uncertainties concerning the secrets of its composition, its multiple intentions, and its internal contradictions, which a critical examination of this work reveals.

In fact, however legitimate and rich its information and ingenious reflections are, the Orientalist approach appears too often like the study of a masterpiece viewed through a magnifying glass, where the theme itself, the beauty of the whole, becomes of secondary importance. No doubt there is much to be gleaned from an exacting analysis of the components of the text, and the problems posed by this scrutiny are certainly far from being devoid of interest. The advent of computers has also sparked a proliferation of studies based on cross-referencing certain key words, otherwise almost impossible to find in such a mass, and this fantastic tool has by no means jeopardised the coherence of the whole, quite the contrary. But there is a severe lack in the academic literature, for those who wish to understand the 'phenomenon' of the *Mahābhārata*, of theological, symbolic, initiatic or spiritual references, which would enable its intrinsic richness to be grasped. It is also revealing that due to their training and academic constraints, Indologists carefully avoid all commentary based on a comparison of different religious traditions still alive,[2] and in doing so, they sound as if they are speaking of a world long gone. Similarly, they refer very seldom to the light shed on the epic by Indian sages themselves. Therefore, willing to address this deficiency, we have referred as often as possible to the Hindu tradition itself in an attempt to restore the epic to its proper framework.

Now from the perspective of this tradition, everything fits. The *Mahābhārata* offers a rereading of the Vedic heritage and reorganises the ancient pantheon while neutralising, if one may so express it, a Buddhism which, in the opinion of the Brahmins, was nothing more than a heresy. It redefines the *sanātana-dharma*, the perennial tradition, by means of the concept, new to the Indian world, of the *avātara,* a descent of God on earth in human form. This descent is required because of an eschatological urgency, as Kṛṣṇa explains when he says that because of the emergence of *adharma* he is made

---

2 Aside from a few references here and there they do not encroach on the realm of comparative religion. An author like Ananda K. Coomaraswamy, whose writings are an inexhaustible mine of cross-references from one spiritual tradition to another, and whose knowledge of Hinduism and Buddhism is exceptionally great is, significantly, very rarely quoted by Orientalists. Unfortunately for our purposes, he did not write much on the *Mahābhārata*.

manifest (cf. ch. 7; *Bhagavad-gītā*, 4, 7). What is more, this urgency demands a more simplified relationship with the divine order to counteract the drift of humanity, which has lost its sense of the sacred and is moving away towards a 'centrifugal' periphery. This new link[3] is the way of *bhakti*, devotion and the renunciation of the fruits of all action. The central cult of *pūjā*, which now replaces the Vedic sacrifice,[4] culminates in the worship of the avatar and the invocation of his Name, or rather one or other of his Names, whose saving power is exalted. To the extent, then, that the avatar has taken human form, that his deeds have created a mythology, he becomes iconographically representable. The worship that is paid to him involves the creation of images and the religion thus conceived becomes iconic, to use the expression of Angot (cf. ch. 5). At the same time, this phenomenon extends to all the gods of the pantheon, whose role is specified by their postures, clothes and the attributes given to them. A number of them acquire, following on

[3] In other words, this new religion, if one uses this word in the sense of link, stemming from *religare*, to connect. But we should not forget that *religio* may also well come from *relegere*, recollect, and thus cover the notion of tradition and transmission. These two etymologies were already known and used by the ancients, who suggested these two meanings upon which modern philologists remain undecided.

[4] The *Mānavadharmaśāstra* (1, 85–6), which defines *dharma* in each age, assigns asceticism (*tejas*) to the *kṛta-yuga*, knowledge (*jñāna*) to the *tretā-yuga*, sacrifice (*yajña*) to the *dvāpara-yuga*, and the gift (*dāna*) to the *kali-yuga*. The gift in question is not so much liberality, as Loiseleur-Deslongchamps has translated, or a humanistic generosity, but rather the gift of the self to the divinity demanded by *bhakti* and culminating in the *pūjā*.

from this, the possibility of becoming *iṣṭa-devatā*, that is to say, divinities of choice who can be substitutes for the avatar as manifestations or emanations of the supreme Divinity, *brahman*. The presence of these images, usually sculptures, demand in their turn the building of temples, unknown in the Vedic period, to serve as their homes. These temples are, what is more, located in precise places, in relation to events recounted firstly in the *Mahābhārata*, then in the *Rāmāyaṇa* and subsequently in all the Puranic literature. By their presence they sanctify the whole land of India and have become the focus of pilgrimages. The sanctification of space is thus connected to a specific situation in time according to the doctrine of the four ages. And we have seen how the architecture of the temple reflects a spatio-temporal concern.

This naturally explains the emergence of two main gods who played only a subsidiary role in the Vedic period: Viṣṇu and Śiva. The first god, who measures the sacrificial space, in other words, the world, in his three strides (a myth later found in the mythology of his incarnation as the dwarf Vāmana), and whose main function is to maintain and preserve *dharma*, asserts himself primarily as the master of space. 'Primarily' because, to the extent that he is an emanation of the supreme divinity, he also has a Śaivite role: 'I am Time, which in progressing destroys the world. I am here-below occupied in destroying men. Even without you, [O Arjuna] none of the warriors arrayed here on the front line of battle shall live,' Kṛṣṇa also says (*Bhagavad-gītā*, 11, 32). But his first concern is to maintain *dharma* by means of the coronation of a *dharmarājan* who can pacify the earth. The second, Śiva, the destroyer and transformer, who orders the ineluctable succession of cosmic cycles, is the master of time.[5] These two gods are both opposed and complementary at the same time, which is indicated by their alternating appearances throughout the events which precede, make up and follow the war of Kurukṣetra.

Some may reproach us, no doubt, for having been too schematic in this overview, but we do not believe a Hindu would refute this simple and synthetic way of showing the coherence of the *Mahābhārata* and that of the religion that it instituted, or at least to which it lent the help of its multifaceted teachings, in perfect harmony with that cornerstone of its construction which is the *Bhagavad-gītā*. In describing the epic as apocalyptic (ch. 2), Biardeau was not wrong, but such a rapprochement with the Judaeo-Christian world cannot be limited only to the historical and literary plane: such a total revolution in the beliefs and religious practices of a civilisation, with the treasures of sanctity that it has given rise to, remains in reality more difficult to explain through the accidental success of a purely human activity, however much that activity was the product of a 'genius', than by its having recourse to a supernatural revelation plunging its roots in the divine source. The great body of believers cannot doubt the assertion that Kṛṣṇa is the imperishable Self (*avyayātman*) without beginning (*aja*, literally without birth) and the Principle of all things. The Hindus have a total faith in the avatar when he says

---

5 Curiously, it took time for the evidence of the complementary functions of Viṣṇu and Śiva to take hold among the Orientalists, and it was Madeleine Biardeau who put an end to the debate, as we have seen above (ch. 6).

to Arjuna that he has taught him the same *yoga*, the same way that he had already taught 'before time', as Sénart glosses, to Vivasvat, the direct ancestor of Manu, the founder of present day humanity (*Bhagavad-gītā*, 4, 1–6). This *yoga*, even if it has been updated to take into account the new cyclic conditions, is thus, for the devotee, a reminder of timeless truths.

The symbolical and didactic values of the *Mahābhārata* are, in the final analysis, the only guarantors of its spiritual efficacy, and thus have assured it both its longevity and universality. In founding the cult of Kṛṣṇa opening onto a transcendence which delivers from the illusion of *saṃsāra*, the *Bhagavad-gītā* provides the only absolutely necessary key to understanding the *Mahābhārata*. One inevitably thinks of Arjuna, who chooses the unique help of the avatar's person leaving the latter's whole army to his enemy. For the devotee, the *bhakta*, the presence of Kṛṣṇa is enough, and he leaves the arsenal of discursive knowledge with the sophisticated speculations of its scholars to Duryodhana, the incarnation of Kali. Not that he despises them, for the heritage of the avatar is in fact twofold. In a neutrality that is situated beyond the cosmic play, Kṛṣṇa abstains from fighting and he says: 'The same I am to all beings; to Me there is none hateful or dear; but whoso worships Me with devotion, they are in Me and I am also in them' (*Bhagavad-gītā* 9, 29). For the Hindu there remains only this truth: *yataskṛṣṇastato jayaḥ*, 'where there is Kṛṣṇa, there is victory.'

Glossary of Main Characters and Sanskrit Terms

Abhimanyu: The Proud, The Enthusiastic. Son of Arjuna and Subhadrā, he dies heroically during the war at the age of sixteen, leaving his wife Uttarā pregnant. He is the incarnation of Soma.

adharma: disorder, confusion. *Adharma* is the opposite of *dharma*.

adharmika: related to *adharma*.

ādivāsī: indigenous people. Name given to the first inhabitants of India, before any invasion or migration. They represent eight per cent of the population of present day India and are not Hindus.

Agni: Fire. Vedic god.

Ahalyā: She who must not be ploughed (?). Name of the wife of the sage Gautama, seduced by Indra.

ahiṃsa: non-violence.

aja: unborn.

Ambā: The Mother. Daughter of the king of Kāśi (Benares) and older sister of Ambikā and Ambālikā. Fell in love with Bhīṣma, was rejected by him because of the vow he had made not to have a woman. She determined to have her revenge and was reborn as

Śikhaṇḍinī, then changed sex to become the warrior Śikhaṇḍin.

Ambālikā: diminutive of mother. Sister of Ambā and Ambikā. Second wife of the son of Śāntanu and Satyavatī. She conceived Pāṇḍu with Vyāsa.

Ambikā: diminutive of mother. First wife of the son of Śāntanu and Satyavatī. She conceived Dhṛtarāṣṭra with Vyāsa.

aṃśa: portion.

Ananta: The Infinite. Name of the serpent Śeṣa.

ānṛśaṃsya: absence of cruelty.

anṛta: lie.

anukrośa: compassion.

apradakṣiṇa: polar direction with the centre on the left (anti-clockwise direction).

araṇya: forest.

Arjuna: The Brilliant, The Silver One. Son of Kuntī and the god Indra, he is the third Pāṇḍava.

artha: material well-being, riches, health.

āśrama: literally effort. Period in life (there are four).

asura: demon.

aśvamedha: horse sacrifice.

Aśvatthāman: Strong as a Horse. Name of Drona's son. He is an incarnation of Rudra, a terrifying form of Śiva.

Aśvin: The Horsemen. Twin gods, bringers of wealth, who perform the role of doctors to the gods.

ātman: reflexive pronoun. The divine Self and the individual self.

avatāra: descent; incarnation.

avyaya: imperishable.

ayana: way.

bala: force.

Balarāma: Rāma the Powerful. Elder brother of Kṛṣṇa, he shares with him the rank of eighth avatar of Viṣṇu or, more precisely, he embodies Śeṣa, the serpent on which Viṣṇu reclines. He remains neutral in the Kurukṣetra war.

bhāga: portion; offering.

Bhagavat: The Fortunate, The Prosperous, The Adorable, The Lord. Name of Kṛṣṇa. The *Bhagavad-gītā* is, literally, the Song of the Lord.

bhakta: faithful, devotee; adherent of *bhakti-yoga*.

bhakti: sharing; love, devotion.

bhakti-yoga: path of love or devotion.

Bhārata: name of the descendants of Bharata, the eponymous ancestor of the Indians.

bhava: state, birth.

bhāva: being, existence; emotion, sentiment.

Bhaya: Fear personified.

Bhīma: The Terrible. Son of Kuntī and the god Vāyu, he is the second of the Pāṇḍava.

Bhīṣma: The Terrible. Son of Śāntanu and Gaṅgā, he received this name because of the terrible nature of his double vow to relinquish power and women. He remains faithful to the Kaurava clan despite his affection for the Pāṇḍava.

bhoktṛ: enjoyer.

bhūta: element (ether, air, fire, water, earth).

Brahmā: The Creator. First god of the Hindu *trimūrti*.

brahman: sacred utterance; absolute, infinite. This term in the neuter gender refers to the supreme Reality.

brāhmaṇa: Brahmin, priest; member of the highest caste.

brahmavādin: formulator and pronouncer of the sacred word.

brahma-vidyā: knowledge of *brahman*.

Bṛhadaśva: He who has a big horse. Name of a sage.

Bṛhaspati: The Master of Prayer. Name of the gods' chaplain and the planet Jupiter.

Buddha: The Awakened One; Gautama Buddha, the historical Buddha, regarded by Hindus as an *avatāra* of Viṣṇu.

buddhi: intellect, intelligence.

Candra: The Ashes, the Moon god. Ancestor of the lunar dynasty.

daiva: destiny.

dakṣa: skilled.

Dakṣa: The Skilful One, ritual Art personified.

dāna: gift.

daṇḍa: stick; punishment.

daṇḍa-nīti: repressive politics.

darśana: vision, point of view; philosophical school.

deva: celestial being, god, angel.

Devakī: The Divine; The Dice Player. Name of Kṛṣṇa's mother.

Devakī-putra: Son of Devakī. Name of Kṛṣṇa.

Devī: the Goddess. Generic name of the deity conceived as female, worshipped in the Śaktik and Tantric sects.

dharba: sacred plant used in certain brahmanic rites. Also called *kuśa*.

dharma: order, law, justice, honour. This term is the etymological equivalent of the Latin *firmus*, firm.

Dharma: the cosmic order personified.

dharmarājan: king conforming to *dharma*.
dharmika: conforming to *dharma*.
Dhaumya: Smoky. Chaplain to the Pāṇḍava.
Dhṛṣṭadyumna: The Dazzling One. Putative son of King Drupada, he arose from the sacrificial fire at the same time as his twin sister Draupadī. He incarnates Agni and is the commander-in-chief of the Pāṇḍava army.
Dhṛtarāṣṭra: He who has a strong empire. Son of Vyāsa and Ambikā. A blind king, married to Gāndhāri, he is the leader of the Kaurava, but is under the control of his son Duryodhana.
dīkṣita: officiator (of the sacrifice); initiate.
Draupadī: the daughter of King Drupada. She was born of the sacrificial fire at the same time as her twin brother, Dhṛṣṭadyumna, and incarnates the Earth and the goddess Śrī. Her own given name is Kṛṣṇā.
Droṇa: The Wooden Container. Name of the Brahmin guru of the young Pāṇḍava and Kaurava. He fights on the latter's side and is the father of Aśvatthāman. He is the embodiment of Bṛhaspati, the priest of the gods.
Drupada: The Trunk, The Pillar of Wood. Name of the putative father of Draupadī and Dhṛṣṭadyumna.
Duḥśāsana: The Evil Councillor. Name of the second of Dhṛtarāṣṭra's hundred sons, who is the evil genius of his elder brother Duryodhana.
Duryodhana: The One Hard to Fight. Name of the eldest son of Gāndhārī and Dhṛtarāṣṭra and the real leader of the Kaurava. He incarnates the *kali-yuga*.
dvāpara-yuga: the age designated by the number two. The third age of the *mahāyuga*, equivalent to the Bronze Age.

Dyu (Dyaus): Heaven personified.

Gāndhārī: The Afghan, the woman who comes from Gandhāra. Name of Dhṛtarāṣṭra's wife and mother of the Kaurava.

Gaṇeśa: The Lord of the Group. Son of Parvatī, god with an elephant's head.

Gaṅgā: The Fluid One. Name of the goddess of the Ganges. Śāntanu's lover and mother of Bhīṣma.

gītā: song, poem.

gopī: gopi, milkmaid, female cowherd.

grāma: village.

Guḍākeśa: He who has thick locks of hair. Name of Arjuna.

guṇa: bowstring; fundamental quality of nature. They are three in number: *sattva*, the good, luminous and ascendent quality; *rajas*, the expansive, passionate and horizontal quality; *tamas*, the obscure, inert and descending quality.

guru: heavy, weighty; venerable, respectable; spiritual master.

Hara: He who takes away. A name of Śiva.

Hari: The Yellow One, The Fawn-coloured One. Name of Kṛṣṇa.

Hāstinapura (Hastināpura): City of the Elephant. Name of the Bhārata capital, situated on the Ganges.

Indra: The Drop of Water. Name of the king of the gods, lord of the rain and thunder.

indriya: sense; organ of perception or action.

iṣṭa-devatā: chosen deity.

īśvara: powerful; Lord, God.

itihāsa: 'he spoke thus'; generic name for the Indian epics.

Janamejaya: He who makes men tremble. Name of Parikṣit's son. It is to him that the story of the *Mahābhārata* is recounted for the first time.

japa-yoga: yoga of continuous invocation.

jāti: birth; caste in the socio-professional context. There are between three and five thousand *jāti* in India.

jyotiṣa: astronomy.

kāla-vañcana: outwitting time.

kali: the number one, which represents the worst throw of the dice.

Kālī: The Black One. Name of Devī; another name of Satyavatī.

Kāliya: The Black One. Name of a serpent which haunted the Yamunā and that Kṛṣṇa tamed in his childhood.

kali-yuga: the age of the worst throw of the dice; the age of conflicts. The Fourth Age of the *mahāyuga*, equivalent to the Iron Age.

Kalki: The Dirty One. Name of the last *avatāra* of Viṣṇu, who must appear at the end of the present *mahāyuga*. He is depicted as a horseman brandishing a sword or as a man with a horse's head.

kalpa: immense time period, equivalent to one day of Brahmā or fourteen *manvantara*.

kāma: love, affection.

Kaṃsa: The (metal) Cup. Name of a treacherous king of Mathurā who imprisoned his father Ugrasena. He did everything he could to prevent the birth of Kṛṣṇa, who escaped from him and eventually killed him.

karma-yoga: sacrificial way, way of works.

karman: act, sacrificial act.

Karṇa: The Ear. Eldest son of Kuntī and Sūrya (the Sun). He got his name from the fact that he was born with a gold breastplate and earrings.

Kaurava: descendants of Kuru. Although the Pāṇḍava are also descendants of Kuru, in the *Mahābhārata* the word only means the sons of Dhṛtarāṣṭra and their allies.

kāvya: classical sanskrit poetry.

Keśava: He who has beautiful hair. Name of Kṛṣṇa.

Kṛṣṇa: The Blue-black One. Kṛṣṇa is the eighth major incarnation of Viṣṇu. Arjuna is also sometimes referred to by this name.

Kṛṣṇā: feminine form of the preceding word. Name of Draupadī.

Kṛṣṇa Dvaipāyana: The Island-born Kṛṣṇa. Name of Vyāsa.

kṛta-yuga: the perfect age. First age of the *mahāyuga*, the equivalent of the Golden Age.

kṣātradharma: rule of warfare.

kṣatriya: man of the (battle) field, warrior; member of the second caste.

kṣetra: battlefield; the world as an object of knowledge.

kṣetrajña: knower of the field.

Kuntī: The Woman of the people of Kunti. Sister of Vāsudeva; Kṛṣṇa's aunt; adopted daughter of Kuntibhoja, wife of Pāṇḍu, mother of Karṇa and the three eldest Pāṇḍava. According to the *Bhāgavatapurāṇa* she is an incarnation of Siddhi (Realisation), the daughter of Dakṣa.

Kuntibhoja: Joy of the Kunti. Name of the king of the Kunti people in present day Gujarat and adoptive father of Kuntī.

Kuru: eponymous ancestor of the Kaurava.

Kurukṣetra: The Field of the Kuru. Site of the battle in the *Mahābhārata*, located on the plains between the Ganges and Yamunā.

kuśa: cf. *dharba*.

Lakṣmī: The Fortunate. Wife of Viṣṇu.

Mādhava: The Honey One. Name of Kṛṣṇa.

Mādrī: The Woman of the people of Madra. Pāṇḍu's second wife and mother of Nakula and Sahadeva.

mahāyuga: cycle of four ages corresponding to the Golden, Silver, Bronze and Iron Ages of the Greek tradition.

manas: internal sense, mental faculty.

Māṇḍavya: Son of Maṇḍu. Name of a *ṛṣi*.

Manu: The Intelligent, The Man. Father of the human race, comparable to Adam. Every *manvantara* is inaugurated by the appearance of a new Manu.

manvantara: era of Manu. An era of Manu or *manvantara* is equal, according to some, to a *mahāyuga*, a cycle of four ages. More often one considers that 71 cycles of 4 ages are necessary to complete one single *manvantara*.

mara: death

mārga: path, track followed by a hunter, spiritual path. Synonymous with *yoga*.

Mārkaṇḍeya (uncertain etymology): Name of a well-known *ṛṣi* who lived for a long time and received a famous vision.

Mathurā (uncertain meaning): Name of the city where Kṛṣṇa was born in the kingdom usurped by Kaṃsa. Mathurā is located on the Yamunā, downstream of Delhi.

matsya: fish

Matsya: name of the kingdom of the Virāṭa; constellation of Pisces.

matsya-nyāya: law of the fish.

māyā: measurement; magic, power of illusion.

mithyāvadha: treachery.

Mitra: The Friend. Vedic god of a sacerdotal nature often associated with Varuṇa.

mokṣa: deliverance. Fourth goal of human existence.

Naimiṣa: lit. (like) the blink of an eye. Name of the forest where the *sattra* takes place during which the *Mahābhārata* is recounted for the first time.

nakṣatra: star; zodiacal constellation (27 in number by which one observes the passage of the moon).

Nakula: The Mongoose. Son of Mādrī and the Aśvin gods. Twin brother of Sahadeva and the fourth Pāṇḍava.

Nanda: Joy, Happiness. Name of the adoptive father of Kṛṣṇa.

Nara: The Man. Name of an ancient *ṛṣi* whose association with Nārāyaṇa prefigures that of Arjuna and Kṛṣṇa.

Nārada: He who teaches men. Name of a divine *ṛṣi*, poet and messenger between men and gods.

Nārāyaṇa: He who is a way for men, or (hermeneuticaly) He who is reclining on the waters (of the cosmic ocean). Name of Viṣṇu.

nīla: blue.

nimeṣa: blink of an eye; a measure of time equalling 0.17 of a second.
niṣkāma-karman: selfless action.

Pāṇḍava: descendant of Pāṇḍu.
Pāṇḍu: The Pale One. Son of Vyāsa and Ambālikā. Husband of Kuntī and Mādrī, putative father of the Pāṇḍava.
para: other; supreme, transcendant.
parama: supreme, transcendant.
Parāśara: The Crusher, The Destroyer. Brahmin father of Vyāsa.
Paraśurāma: Rāma of the Axe. Sixth major incarnation of Viṣṇu.
Parikṣit: He who remains, surrounds. Name of the son of Arjuna and Subhadrā. Foremost heir of the Pāṇḍava. Written as Parīkṣit, this name means He who examines.
Parvatī: She who runs like a cascade. Name of Śiva's wife.
phala-tṛṣṇa-vairāgya: renunciation of the fruits of action.
Phālguna: Born under Phalgunī. Name of Arjuna.
Phalgunī: The Tiny One. Name of a constellation.
pitāmaha: grandfather.
pradakṣiṇa: solar direction with the centre on the right (= clockwise).
Prājāpati: The Lord of Creatures.
prakṛti: nature; feminine principle of manifestation (as opposed to *puruṣa*).
pralaya: dissolution.
Pratīpa: the one who walks backwards, The Inverse. Name of Śāntanu's father.
preman: love.

priya: dear.
Pṛthivī: The Spread out One. Name of the goddess Earth.
pūjā: cult, rite of worship.
purāṇa: ancient.
puruṣa: man; male principle of manifestation (as opposed to *prakṛti*).
Puruṣa: The Principial Man whose self-sacrifice and dismemberment creates the world according to Vedic doctrine.
puruṣārtha: goal of life (four in number).

Rādhā: Prosperity, Success. Name of Kṛṣṇa's favourite lover in the *Gīta-Govinda* by Jayadeva (12th century).
Rādhā: Adhiratha's wife and foster mother of Karṇa.
Rāma: The Pleasant One, The Charming One, (etymologically: The Black One). Name of three successive *avatāra* of Viṣṇu: Paraśurāma (Rāma with an axe), Rāmacandra (the lunar Rāma, hero of the *Rāmāyaṇa*) and Balarāma (the strong Rāma), the elder brother of Kṛṣṇa.
Rāmacandra: The Lunar Rāma, hero of the *Rāmāyaṇa*.
Rohinī: The Red Cow. Second wife of Vasudeva and mother of Balarāma.
ṛṣi: seer; poet, prophet.
Rudra: The Howler. Name of Śiva.
rūpa: form; beauty.

Sahadeva: With the Gods. Son of Mādrī and the Aśvin gods. Twin brother of Nakula and the fifth Pāṇḍava.
śakti: energy, power.
Śakuni: The Bird (of Doom). Brother of Gāndhārī and uncle of the Kaurava. He embodies the *dvāpara-yuga*.

Śalya: The Arrow. Mādrī's brother and last general of the Kaurava.

Sāṃkhya: enumeration. Name of one of the six *darśana*, or perspectives, of Indian philosophy.

saṃsāra: flux (of existence); the world.

saṃskṛta: completed, perfect; name of the language described by Pāṇini.

sanātana-dharma: perennial order, (Hindu) tradition.

Sañjaya: The Victorious. Name of the charioteer who tells the blind Dhṛtarāṣṭra what is happening in the war.

Śāntanu: The Handsome One. King of the Kuru. First, as lover of Gaṅgā, he begets Bhīṣma with her. Then as Satyavatī's husband, he begets two sons who die young and childless.

śarīra: body.

sattra: Vedic sacrifice.

sattva: conforming to being, good; quality of nature, *guṇa*.

Satyavatī: The Truthful One. Daughter of the king of the fish. Mother of Vyāsa, from a union in her youth with the Brahmin Parāśara; later wife of Śāntanu, to whom she gives two sons who die young and childless.

Śaunaka: Son of a Dog. Name of the leader of the Vedic sacrifice where the *Mahābhārata* is recounted.

Śeṣa: The Remainder. Name of the cosmic serpent upon which Viṣṇu Nārāyaṇa reclines; incarnated as Balarāma.

Sītā: The Furrow. Wife of Rāmacandra and incarnation of Lakṣmī.

Śiva: The Propitious One. Third god of the *trimūrti*.

śloka: verse, stanza.

smṛti: memory; category of traditional writings.
soma: strong drink, nectar; Vedic god.
śruti: audition; category of traditional writings.
Subhadrā: The Glorious One, The Auspicious One. Sister of Kṛṣṇa; Arjuna's wife; mother of Abhimanyu. She incarnates *yoga-nidrā*, The Sleep of *yoga*.
śūdra: servant; member of the fourth caste.
sura: celestial being, god.
Sūrya: the Sun. Father of Karṇa.
sūta: charioteer. Charioteers were often bards.
svadharma: personal *dharma* belonging to each individual.
svastika: lit. happiness. Cross prolonged by perpendicular bars. The *svastika* can be *pradakṣiṇa* or *apradakṣiṇa*, according to whether it is showing a solar or polar movement.

tamas: dark; quality of nature, *guṇa*.
tejas: heat; ascesis.
tretā-yuga: the age designated by the number three. Second age of the *mahāyuga*, equivalent to the Silver Age.
trimūrti: triple manifestation.

udgītha: technical name for the psalmody of the *Sāmaveda*, the *Veda* of chants.
Ugraśravas: He who has heard (or makes people hear) terrible things. Name of the charioteer who recounts the *Mahābhārata* in the forest of Naimiṣa.
Upamanyu: The Zealous, The Intelligent. Disciple of a sage healed of his blindness by the Aśvin.
upāya: ruse.

Vaiśampāyana: Son of the Protector of People. Name of the disciple of Vyāsa who tells the story of the *Mahābhārata* to Janamejaya.

vaiśya: peasant, herder, artisan, merchant; member of the third caste.

Vaivasvata: The Son of the Sun (Vivasvat). Proper name of the Manu of the present *manvantara*.

Vālmīki: He who is covered in ants. Name of the author of the *Rāmāyaṇa*.

Vāmana: The Dwarf. Name of the fifth major incarnation of Viṣṇu.

varṇa: colour; caste in the socio-religious context. The *varṇa* are four in number.

Varuṇa: The Encompasser. Multifunctional Vedic god often associated with Mitra.

vāstu-puruṣa-maṇḍala: square of the abode of man. Foundation plan of a temple.

vasu: good, beneficent; shining.

Vasudeva: The Bright Celestial Being. Husband of Devakī and father of Kṛṣṇa.

Vāsudeva: Son of Vasudeva. Name of Kṛṣṇa.

Vāyu: the Wind. Father of Bhīma.

vedāṅga: a 'limb' of the *Veda*; generic name for the six traditional sciences connected to the study of the *Veda*.

Vedānta: the end of the *Veda* (= *Upaniṣad*); name of one of the six *darśana* or perspectives of Indian philosophy.

vedī: altar for the Vedic sacrifices.

Vicitravīrya: The Shining Hero. Name of the second son of Śāntanu and Satyavatī, who died without any descendants.

Vidura: The Intelligent One, The Skilful One. Third son of Vyāsa. Half-brother of Dhṛtarāṣṭra and Pāṇḍu. Incarnation of Dharma.

Virāṭa: He who rules over a large kingdom. Name of the king of the Matsya in whose kingdom the Pāṇḍava must live incognito in their thirteenth year of exile.

Viṣṇu: The Penetrating One. Second god of the *trimūrti*.

Vivasvat: The Shining One. Name of the Sun.

Vṛndāvana: The Great Forest. Forest where Kṛṣṇa lives in his youth near Mathurā.

Vṛṣṇi: The Powerful One, The Mighty One. Name of the eponymous king of the Vṛṣṇi, the descendants of Yādava.

Vṛtra: The Embracer. Mythic serpent or dragon killed by Indra.

Vyāsa: The Diffuser, The Compiler. The title of Kṛṣṇa Dvaipāyana, the author of the *Mahābhārata*.

vyāsa-kūṭa: enigmas of Vyāsa; enigmatic verses dictated by Vyāsa to Gaṇeśa.

Yādava: descendant of Yadu. Name of a people and name of Kṛṣṇa.

Yadu (uncertain meaning): ancestor of the Yādava, of the non-reigning branch of the lunar dynasty.

yajña: sacrifice.

Yama: He who holds (the leashes), He who binds. God of death.

Yamunā: sister of Yama, the god of death. Tributary of the Ganges, now the Jumnā.

yantra: bond; machine; body; sacred diagram.

Yaśodā: She that gives glory. Wife of Nanda, foster mother of Kṛṣṇa.

Yavana: Ionian, Greek.
yoga: yoke; union; spiritual path.
Yudhiṣṭhira: He who is firm in combat. Son of Kuntī and the god Dharma. Oldest brother of the Pāṇḍava.
yuga: age, cyclic period.
yukta: team of horses or other animals.
Yuyutsu: the only son of Dhṛtarāṣṭra who takes the side of the Pāṇḍava. His mother is a *vaiśya* woman.

Genealogical Tables of the Principal Characters in the *Mahābhārata*

In the following tables the names of the male heroes are in Roman characters; the heroines are given in italics; the gods and goddesses are highlighted in capital letters and the eponyms are found in bold.

—The Yādava (descendants of Yadu), the Paurava (descendants of Pūru), the Kaurava (descendants of Kuru) and the Pāṇḍava (descendants of Pāṇḍu), all belong to the lunar dynasty, which means their common ancestor is the god Candra (or Soma), the Moon. The latter had an illegitimate son by Tārā, the wife of his guru Bṛhaspati (Jupiter); their son is called Budha (Mercury). [Not to be confused with Buddha!]

—The term 'Kaurava' is ambiguous. Etymologically, it signifies all the descendants of Kuru, the grandfather of Śāntanu. The Pāṇḍava are also, technically speaking, Kaurava. But as used in the epic, the name Kaurava only applies to the sons of Dhṛtarāṣṭra.

—Some important characters in the *Mahābhārata* do not belong to the lunar dynasty (or are only connected indirectly by marriage):

a. Vyāsa, the biological father of Dhṛtarāṣṭra, Pāṇḍu,

Vidura and Śuka, is a Brahmin. His father, Parāśara, is a descendant of the god Brahmā and his mother, Satyavatī, is a daughter of Matsya, the king of the Fish. It should be noted that the main characters in the epic, the Pāṇḍava and the Kaurava, only belong to the lunar dynasty in an indirect manner and, what is more, the five Pāṇḍava, are actually the sons of different gods. But Abhimanyu (and consequently his own descendants beginning with Parikṣit) have lunar blood in their veins by his mother Subhadrā, Kṛṣṇa's sister.

b. Droṇa and his son Aśvatthāman are also Brahmins.

c. In the same way, Ambā, Ambikā and Ambālikā, the daughters of the king of Kāśī (Benares); Gāndhārī and Śakuni, the children of Subala, the king of Gandhāra; and Mādrī, the daughter of Śalya, the king of Madra, in the north-west of Hindustan, are only connected to the lunar dynasty by marriage.

d. In contrast, Draupadī and her twin brother Dhṛṣṭadyumna, are born of the sacrificial fire and thus Agni. But as the adopted children of king Drupada, they are Paurava. Drupada in fact belongs to a branch of the family descended from Bharata (but not from Kuru).

1. The Lunar Dynasty

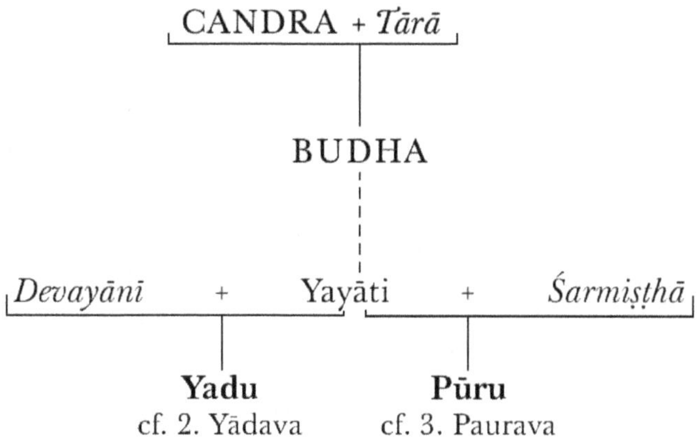

2. Genealogy of the Yādava

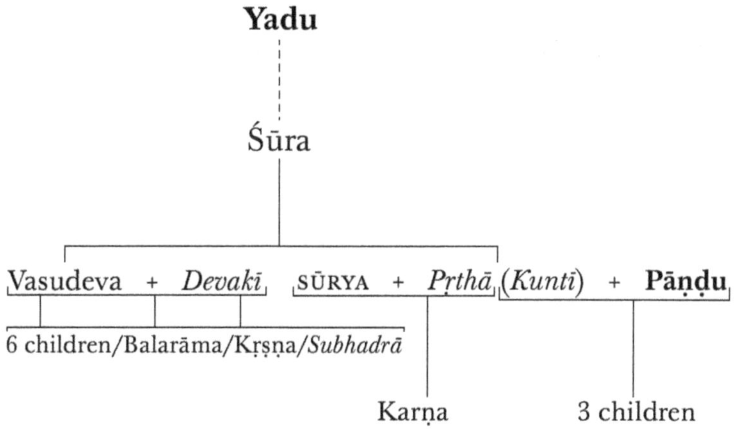

3. Genealogy of the Paurava

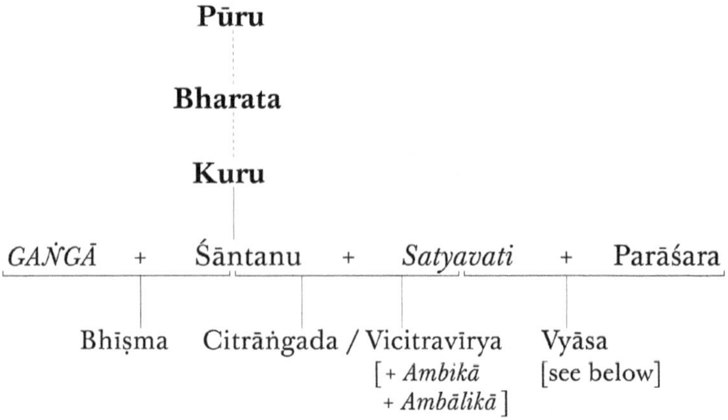

4. Descendants of Vyāsa

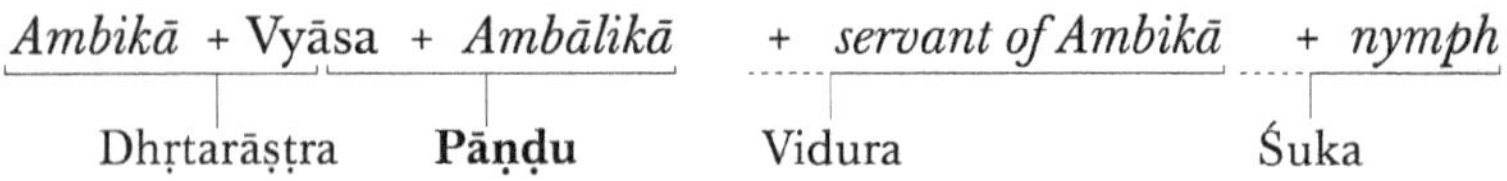

5. Genealogy of the Kaurava

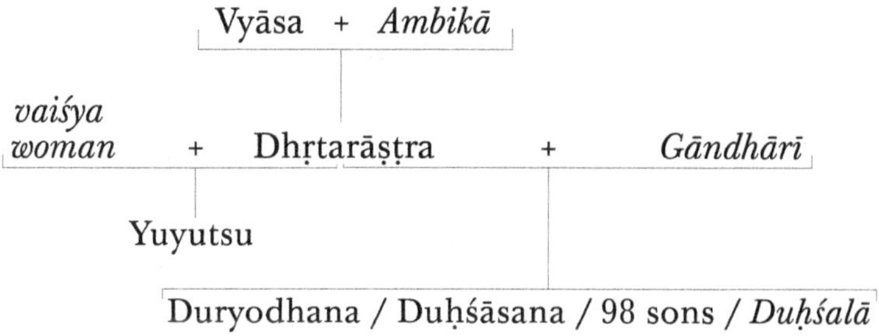

6. Genealogy of the Pāṇḍava

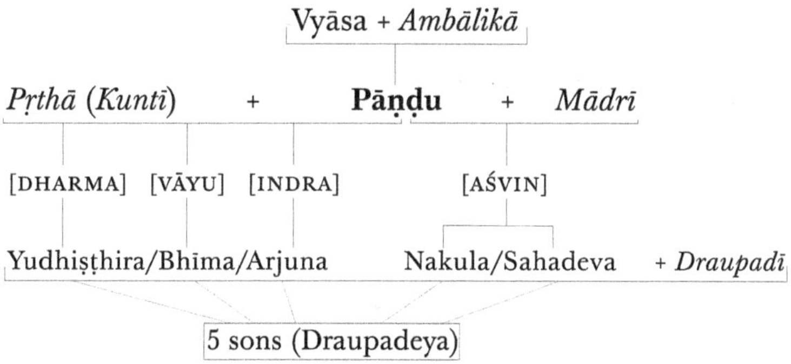

7. Descendants of Arjuna

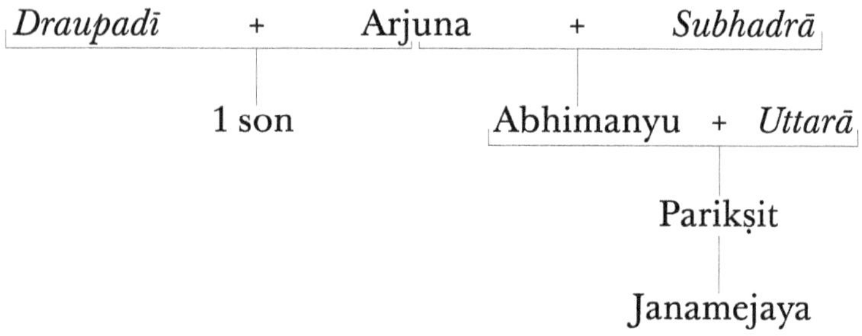

Bibliography

Angot, Michel, *L'Inde classique*, Les Belles Lettres, Paris, 2001.

Biardeau, Madeleine, 1985: cf. Péterfalvi Jean-Michel.

Biardeau, Madeleine, *Le Mahābhārata, un récit fondateur du brahmanisme et son interprétation*, éditions du Seuil, Paris, 2002 (2 vols).

Bronkhorst, Johannes, *Aux origines de la philosophie indienne*, Infolio, Gollion, 2008.

Buck, William, *Mahabharata*, Penguin Books Ltd, 1992.

Burckhardt, Titus, *Foundations of Oriental Art & Symbolism*, World Wisdom, Bloomington, 2009.

Carrière, Jean-Claude, *Le Mahabharata*, éditions Belfond, 1989.

Carrière, Jean-Claude, *Dictionnaire amoureux de l'Inde*, Plon, Paris, 2001.

Chevalier, Jean and Gheerbrant, Alain, *Dictionnaire des symboles*, Robert Laffont/Jupiter, Paris, [1969] 1982.

Chidbhavananda, Swami, *The Bhagavad Gita*, Sri Ramakrishna Tapovanam, Tiruchirappalli, 1969.

Coomaraswamy, Ananda K., *Spiritual Authority and Temporal Power in the Indian Theory of Government,* Munshiram Manoharlal, Delhi, [1942] 1978.

Coomaraswamy, Ananda K., *Pour comprendre l'art hindou*, éditions AWAC, Le Haut Blosne- Rennes, 1979.

Coomaraswamy, Ananda K., *Hinduism and Buddhism*, Indira Gandhi National Centre for the Arts, New Delhi, 1999.

Daniélou, Alain, *The Myths and Gods of India: the Classic work on Hindu Polytheism*, from the Princeton Bollingen Series, Inner Traditions/Bear and Co, 1991.

Daumal, René, *Bharata, L'Origine du théâtre, la poésie et la musique en Inde*, Gallimard, Paris, 1970.

Demetrian, Serge, *Le Mahâbhârata conté selon la tradition orale*, Albin Michel, Paris, 2006.

Diogenes Laertius, *Lives of Eminent Philosophers*, R. D. Hicks, Ed. Online edition at Tufts University Perseus Project (www.perseus.tufts.edu).

Droit, Roger-Pol, *L'oubli de l'Inde, Une amnésie philosophique*, Editions du Seuil, Paris, 2004.

Dumézil, Georges, *Mythe et épopée, l'idéologie des trois fonctions dans les épopées des peuples indo-européens*, vol. 1, Gallimard, Paris, [1968] 1986[5].

Dumézil, Georges, *The Destiny of the Warrior*, trans. Alf Hiltebeitel, University of Chicago Press, Chicago and London, 1970.

Dutt, Romesh C., *Maha-Bharata, The Epic of Ancient India, Condensed into English Verse*, Kessinger Publishing, 2010.

Eliade, Mircea, *Images and Symbols: Studies in Religious Symbolism*, trans. Philip Mairet, Princeton University Press, 1961.

Feller, Danielle, *The Sanskrit Epics' Representation of Vedic Myths*, Motilal Banarsidass, Delhi, 2004.

Ganguli, Kisari Mohan, *The Mahabharata of Krishna-Dwaipayana Vyasa*, CreateSpace Independent Publishing Platform, 2014.

Georgel, Gaston, *Les quatre Âges de l'humanité*, Archè, Milano, 1976[2].

González-Reimann, Luis, *The Mahābhārata and the Yugas, India's Great Epic Poem and the Hindu System of World Ages*, Peter Lang, New York, 2002 (reprint: Motilal Banarsidass, Delhi, 2010).

Grimal, Pierre, *Romans grecs et latins*, Gallimard, Paris, 1958.

Guénon, René, *Formes traditionnelles et cycles cosmiques*, Gallimard, Paris, 1970.

Guénon, René, *Man and His Becoming According to the Vedânta*, trans. Nicholson, Sophia Perennis, Ghent, NY, 2001.

Guénon, René, *The Reign of Quantity and the Signs of the Times*, translated by Lord Northbourne, Sophia Perennis, Hillsdale NY, 2001.

Guénon, René, *Fragments doctrinaux*, textes rassemblés par Mircea A. Tamas et Gauthier Pierozak, Rose-Cross Books, Toronto, 2013.

Héhaka Sapa, *The Sacred Pipe, Black Elk's account of the Seven Rites of the Oglala Sioux*, recorded and edited by Joseph Epes Brown, Penguin Books, Middlesex, 1971.

Herbert, Jean, *L'Enseignement de Râmakrishna*, Albin Michel, Paris, [1949] 1972.

Hiltebeitel, Alf, *The Cult of Draupadī, 1, Mythologies: From Gingee to Kurukṣetra*, University of Chicago Press, Chicago, 1988.

Hiltebeitel, Alf, *The Ritual of Battle, Krishna in the Mahābhārata*, State University of New York Press, New York, 1990.

Hiltebeitel, Alf, *Rethinking the Mahābhārata, A Reader's Guide to the Education of the Dharma King*, The University of Chicago Press, Chicago, 2001.

Hiltebeitel, Alf, 'Two Kṛṣṇas, Three Kṛṣṇas, Four Kṛṣṇas, More Kṛṣṇas: Dark Interactions in the *Mahābhārata*', in: *Essays on the Mahābhārata*, edited by Arvind Sharma, Motilal Banarsidass, Delhi, 2011, p. 101ff.

Kṛṣṇopaniṣad: English translation from *Sri Krishna Upanisad and Other Vaisnava Upanisads*, retrieved online at http://vedicilluminations.com

Kramrisch, Stella, *The Hindu Temple*, Motilal Banarsidass, Delhi, [1946] 1976 (2 vols).

Lerner, Paule, *Astrological Key in the Mahābhārata, The New Era,* trans. David White, Motilal Benarsidass, Delhi, 1988.

Lings, Martin, *The Secret of Shakespeare*, Quinta Essentia, Cambridge, [1966] 1996.

Lubac, Henri de, *Medieval Exegesis: The Four Senses of Scripture*, 3 vols., trans. M. Sebanc and E. M. Macierowsky, Eerdmans, Grand Rapids, Michigan, 1998–2009.

Mahābhārata: see Biardeau, Buck, Dutt, Ganguli and Gupta, Menon, Narayan, Smith, and Subramanian.

Malinar, Angelika, 'Duryodhana's Truths: Kingship and Divinity', in: *Battle, Bards and Brāhmins*, edited by John Brockington, Motilal Banarsidass, Delhi, 2012.

Menon, Ramesh, *The Mahabharata: A Modern Rendering*, Rupa & co., 2007.

Narayan, R.K., *Mahabharata*, South Asia Books, 1998.

Pernety, Dom Antoine-Joseph, *Les Fables égyptiennes et grecques dévoilées et réduites au même principe, avec une explication des hiéroglyphes et de la guerre de Troye*, Bauche, Paris, 1758.

Perry, Whitall N., *The Widening Breach: Evolutionism in the Mirror of Cosmology*, Quinta Essentia, Cambridge, 1995.

Péterfalvi, Jean-Michel, *Le Mahābhārata, extraits traduits du sanscrit par Jean-Michel Péterfalvi, introduction et commentaires par Madeleine Biardeau*, Flammarion, Paris, 1985–6 (2 vols).

Polier, Antoine-Louis De, *Le Mahabarat et le Bhagavat du colonel De Polier*, présenté par Georges Dumézil, Gallimard, Collection blanche, Paris, 1986.

Prabhupāda, A.C. Bhaktivedanta Swami, *The Nectar of Devotion*, The Bhakti Vedanta Book Trust, London, 1985.

Renou, Louis and Jean Filliozat, *L'Inde classique, manuel des études indiennes*, Maisonneuve, Paris, [1947–49] 1985 (2 vols.).

Rivière, Jean M., *La sainte Upaniṣad de la Bhagavad-gītā*, introduction, commentaire et texte traduit du sanskrit, Archè, Milano, 1979.

Sāṃkhya-kārikā of Isvara Krsna, trans. S. Suryanarayana Sastri, University of Madras, Mylapore, 1930.

Sauge, André, *'L'Iliade', poème athénien de l'époque de Solon*, Peter Lang, Bern, 2000.

Schaufelberger, Gilles and Vincent Guy, *Le Mahābhārata, textes traduits du Sanskrit et annotés*, Presses de l'Université de Laval (Québec), 4 vols., 2004–2009 (cf. www.utqueant.org).

Schuon, Frithjof, *The Transcendent Unity of Religions,* trans. Peter Townsend, Faber and Faber, London, 1953.

Schuon, Frithjof, *The Stations of Wisdom,* translated by G.E.H. Palmer, John Murray, London, 1961.

Schuon, Frithjof, *From the Divine to the Human*, World Wisdom Books, Bloomington, 1982.

Senart, Emile, *La Bhagavad-gîtâ*, SBL, Paris, 1967.

Smith, J.D., *The Mahabharata* abridged, Penguin Classics, 2009.

Subramanian, Kamala, *Mahabharata*, Bharatiya Vidya Bhavan, 2009.

Sukthankar, Vishnu S., *On the Meaning of the Mahabharata*, The Asiatic Society of Bombay, Bombay, [1942] 1957.

Varenne, Jean, *Mythes et légendes extraits des Brâhmanas*, traduits du sanskrit et annotés par J. Varenne, Connaissance de l'Orient, Gallimard/Unesco, Paris, 1967.

Vincent, Guy: see Schaufelberger.

Wiseman, Nicolas, *Discours sur les rapports entre la science et la religion révélée*, Paris, 1845.

Wohlschlag, Dominique, *La Reine et l'avatar, mythologie de Krishna*, Infolio, CH-Gollion, 2013. English translation: *The Queen and the Avatar*, London, The Matheson Trust, 2017.

CPSIA information can be obtained
at www.ICGtesting.com
Printed in the USA
BVHW080937210321
603030BV00005B/729

9 781908 09217